MAY   2000

Norway

Norway

BY
JEAN F. BLASHFIELD

Enchantment of the World
Second Series

Children's Press®

A Division of Grolier Publishing

NEW YORK   LONDON   HONG KONG   SYDNEY
DANBURY, CONNECTICUT

Frontispiece: A Sami child in traditional clothes

Consultant: Ellen Rees, Ph.D., Assistant Professor of Scandinavian Studies, Arizona State University

Please note: All statistics are as up-to-date as possible at the time of publication.

Visit Children's Press on the Internet: http://publishing.grolier.com

Library of Congress Cataloging-in-Publication Data

Blashfield, Jean F.
         Norway / Jean F. Blashfield.
            p. cm. — (Enchantment of the world. Second series)
         Includes bibliographical references and index.
         Summary: Describes the geography, plants and animals, history,
economy, language, religions, culture, sports and arts, and people
of Norway.
         ISBN 0-516-20651-6
         1. Norway Juvenile literature. [1. Norway.] I. Title.
II. Series.
DL409.B58 2000
948.1—dc21   99-21552
                                                                                              CIP

Acknowledgments

Thanks to Anders Aasen, student from Norway, for all his enthusiastic help, and to the Norwegian consuls general in New York City and Minneapolis, Minnesota.

Cover photo:
A stave church

Contents

CHAPTER

Aurora borealis

A seal pup

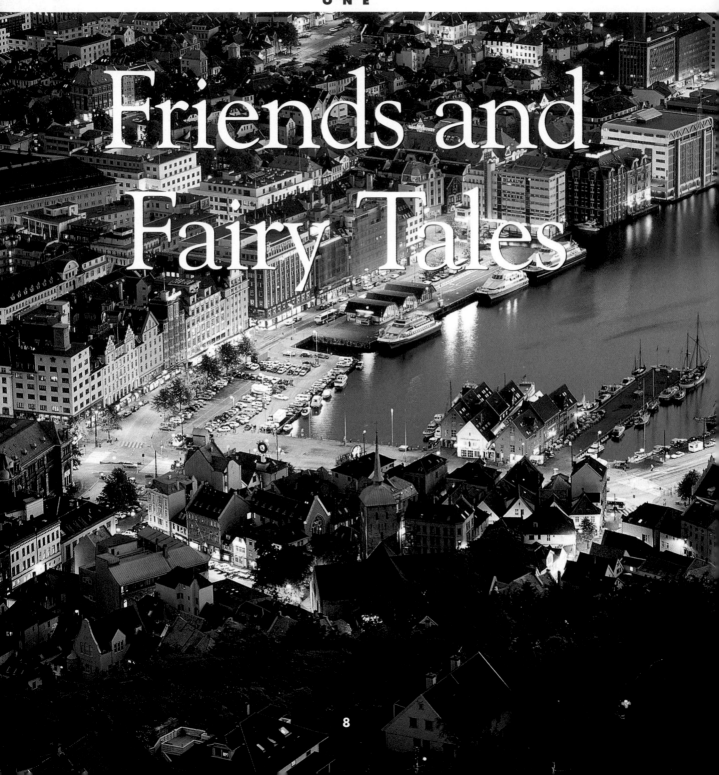

Friends and Fairy Tales

"NORWAY IS A COUNTRY with no enemies and many friends. Some are attracted to Norway by sport; others by the stern beauty of its rockbound coast." These were the first words in a history of Norway written in 1926, and things aren't much different today.

Norway is a land where fairy tales come to life, where the people cherish and enjoy their beautiful countryside. The Norwegians have used their resources to create a way of life that is equal and joyful for everyone.

Norway is a kingdom, officially the Kingdom of Norway, or *Kongeriket Norge*. Its name comes from *Nordweg*, meaning "Northern Way." This name was given to the land by Ottar, a Viking chieftain who visited King Alfred in England about A.D. 880. Alfred had his scribes record what Ottar told him about his northern land, putting down the first written information about Norway.

In ancient times, the homeland of the ferocious Vikings—the Norsemen—was known as Scandinavia. It was an Old Norse name for the peninsula that lies between the North Atlantic and the Gulf of Bothnia. In other words, it includes Norway and Sweden. However, because the histories of

Opposite: **Bergen city and harbor at dusk**

NORWAY
- Cities of over 50,000 people
- Smaller cities and towns
- Administrative centers

0 — 200 miles

0 — 300 kilometers

Geopolitical map
of Norway

Norway, Sweden, and Denmark are intertwined, all three nations are regarded as Scandinavia. Sometimes Finland and Iceland are also included.

Norway is a land of water—glaciers, waterfalls, islands, lakes, rivers, and those glorious sea inlets called fjords. The Norwegian people are natural seafarers. Even the Vikings got their name from the water. *Viking* means "men of the bays."

Today, the Norwegian people are homebodies, completely in love with their own country, yet thoroughly international. Almost nobody else in the world speaks their language so they kindly all learn English. They have made their country into one of the most comfortable places on earth, where they welcome the world.

Reading Names in this Book

The Norwegian language uses three letters—all vowels—that do not occur in English. They are å, ø, and æ. They will appear often in this book in the names of people and places, so it helps to know something about them.

å   is pronounced *oh*. King Håkon is *HOH-kuhn*. Many English people use *aa*, as in *Haakon*, as the translation of the å. But the Norwegians use *aa* only at the beginning of a word.

ø   is pronounced *ir* as a letter. In words, it is pronounced like *worm* or *bird*. Bjørn is a common name.

æ   is pronounced like the *a* in *bat*. The Æsir are a family of gods worshiped by the Vikings.

A Land Created by Ice

O N A MAP, NORWAY LOOKS LIKE A GIANT'S CLUB LYING ALONG- side Sweden, with its wide head to the south and its handgrip reaching into the Arctic Ocean. This long, narrow country stretches from 58 degrees north latitude to almost 72 degrees north. About one-third of it lies north of the Arctic Circle, which is at 66.5 degrees north. Norway also owns islands that reach all the way to 80 degrees north.

The southernmost point on the Norwegian mainland is called the Nape. The northernmost point off Norway's mainland is North Cape. North Cape, like much of Norway, is on an island. The country is only 4 miles (6.4 kilometers) wide at its narrowest point—the Tys Fjord—and 270 miles (435 km) wide at its widest. Following a straight line from north to south, Norway is 1,089 miles (1,753 km) long.

A lighthouse on Henningsvaer Harbor on the Atlantic Ocean

Borders and Seas

Much of Norway is surrounded by sea. The North Atlantic Ocean lies to the west. Above the Arctic Circle, the Atlantic is called the Norwegian Sea, but it has no defining bound- ary. The North Sea lies to the south, with a wide strait called the Skagerrak lying between

Denmark and Norway. The Barents Sea, which is part of the Arctic Ocean, lies to the north. The many deep inlets along the coast, called fjords, make the actual coastline more than 13,000 miles (20,921 km) long. If the islands are included, Norway's coastline is more than 32,000 miles (51,500 km) long.

Norway's Geographical Features

Highest Elevation: Galdhøpiggen, 8,100 feet (2,469 m), Scandinavia's highest point

Lowest Elevation: Sea level along the coast

Longest River: Glåma River, 372 miles (599 km) long

Largest Lake: Lake Mjøsa, 142 square miles (368 sq km)

Coastline: 13,267 miles (21,351 km), including all fjords and peninsulas; about half the distance around the world

Longest Fjord: Sogne Fjord, 110 miles (177 km) long

Largest Glacier: Jostedalsbreen, 188 square miles (487 sq km), largest glacier in Europe

Greatest Distance Northeast to Southwest: 1,089 miles (1,753 km)

Greatest Distance Northwest to Southeast: 270 miles (435 km)

Narrowest Distance: 4 miles (6.4 km)

Land of the Midnight Sun: In northern Norway, the sun does not set from mid-May to the end of July; the sun does not rise above the horizon from the end of November to the end of January.

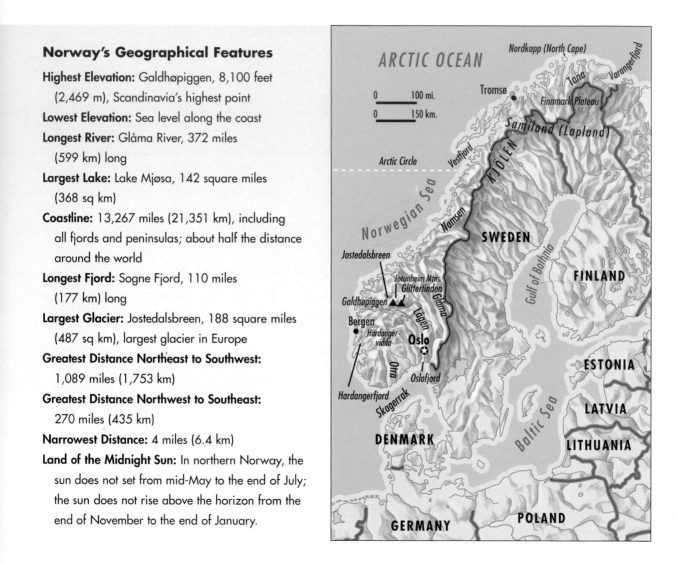

In the east, much of Norway borders Sweden, which owned this land for many years. The northern part of the border between Norway and Sweden is a high, mountainous region called *Kjølen*, meaning "keel." In the north, Norway wraps around northern Finland and then touches Russia.

The area of Norway without its island possessions is 125,191 square miles (324,220 sq km). With a population of 4.4 million, it has a population density of only about 35 people per square mile (13.5 per sq km). In Europe, only Iceland is less densely populated.

Glaciers and Fjords

Once upon a time, a layer of permanent ice, the glaciers, covered almost one-third of the Earth. Those living things that were able to move migrated to the warmer parts of the planet, and the glacial ice lay cold and silent for long millions of years. The ice covering Norway during the Ice Ages of Earth's history may have been 2 miles (3.2 km) thick. The Ice Ages ended when the Earth began to warm and the ice began to melt back toward the Arctic, creating Norway's scenery.

The most spectacular work of the glaciers is the fjords, which cut deeply into the coast of Norway. Fjords are narrow, usually very deep, inlets in which the sea penetrates the land between steep cliffs. There are fjords along Norway's entire coastline. The city of Bergen is called the "Fjord Capital" of Norway.

Norway still has approximately 1,700 glaciers. The edges of these glaciers are constantly melting, turning into water

The Rising Land

During the Ice Ages, so much of Earth's water was bound up in glaciers that the bottom of what is now the North Sea was exposed. The fjords were once river valleys that branched off the exposed land, so some fjords today are deeper than the sea from which they flow. Also, as the glaciers retreated, the land underneath them was relieved of the great weight of ice and it gradually rose, forming the stunning cliffs that border many fjords.

Jostedalsbreen

that drops over any rock edge that it finds. Thousands of glorious waterfalls in Norway are created by melting glaciers.

It seems as if Europe's largest glacier would be in the far north, but it is actually south of Ålesund near the west coast. Called *Jostedalsbreen*, or Jostedals Glacier, this remnant of the Ice Ages covers 188 square miles (487 sq km) and is still growing.

In ancient times, the glaciers carried away soil from mountaintops as they moved over the land. When they retreated, they left land that lay low and flat enough to collect soil. These areas, which can be cultivated today, lie along the Oslo Fjord, around the Trøndelag region, and in the lakes region of the east.

Norway is so rocky, mountainous, forested, and lake-filled that only 3 percent of its land is good farmland. The largest agricultural area is the Jæren Plain, south of Stavanger.

Ice and Water

Norway has so many islands (about 150,000) and lakes (160,000) that it is sometimes difficult to tell where the water ends and the land begins. Only about 2,000 of the islands are inhabited, however.

As the great glaciers retreated, the water level rose, filling in low spots, and the ice carved out spectacular peaks and valleys. It also scraped the tops off some mountains, leaving flat plateaus called *vidder*. A *vidde* is an open area that is usually high and often swampy, similar to an English moor.

Norway's largest lake is Mjøsa, north of Oslo. Eidsvoll, the town where Norway's constitution was signed in 1814, is on the south end of that long lake. Lillehammer, where the 1994 Winter Olympics were held, is at the north end.

Although Norway has many lakes, it has few rivers. Most rivers are in the east, away from fjord country. The only really long river is the Glåma, which is about 372 miles (599 km) long.

The town of Lillehammer

The Sum of Its Parts

Norwegians think of their country as divided into five parts. These are *Nord Norge*, the northern portion; *Trøndelag*, or Mid-Norway, the central section; and three southern portions—*Vestlandet*, the West Country; *Østlandet*, the East Country; and the southernmost part, between Oslo and Stavanger, called *Sørlandet*, the South Country.

Stavanger is now the chief port of the North Sea oil industry, but it used to be an important exit point for emigrants going to the United States. Sørlandet has long, sunny beaches. Inland, it has a few dairy farms.

The southern mountains, called the *Langfjellet*, or Long Mountains, form a huge ridge that divides southern Norway into East Country and West Country. Within this region are

Galdhøpiggen, in Jotunheimen National Park, is the highest peak in Scandinavia.

the *Jotunheim* Mountains, meaning "Home of the Giants," and Jotunheimen National Park. Its highest peak, which is also the highest peak in Scandinavia, is Galdhøpiggen at 8,100 feet (2,469 m). Neighboring Glittertinden is only a few feet shorter.

Also within the Langfjellet is the Hardangervidda Plateau. Hardangervidda National Park covers 3,861 square miles (10,000 sq km) and is home to Europe's largest herd of wild reindeer. It is also home to a major glacier.

Trøndelag, the area around Trondheim, is a land of forests, mines, and fishing. Near Trondheim itself, the land is fairly flat, making it an important agricultural area.

Looking at Norwegian Cities

Bergen, on the North Sea coast, is Norway's second-largest city. Soon after the Viking era, Bergen became the capital of Norway. Much of the old city remains. Bergen still has its historic port and cobblestone streets, and the city is known for the colorful old wooden houses lining its historic wharf. Today, Bergen is the chief seaport of western Norway and carries on trade in dried fish, herring, machinery, and oil. Annual rainfall is a soggy 83 inches (211 centimeters), and temperatures range from 35° Fahrenheit (1.7° Celcius) in January to 60°F (15.6°C) in July.

Trondheim, Norway's third-largest city, lies north of Bergen along Trondheim Fjord. Founded in 997 by King Olav I, the city was Norway's capital until the 1300s. Today, Trondheim factories produce canned goods, building materials, and metal products. Tourists visit Nidaros Cathedral, which is built on the grave of St. Olav. Construction began on the cathedral in 1070. Temperatures range from 26°F (–3.3°C) in January to 57°F (14°C) in July, and annual rainfall is 32 inches (81 cm).

Stavanger (above), Norway's fourth-largest city, lies in southwestern Norway on Stavanger Fjord. Founded in the 700s, Stavanger was the sardine capital of the world in the 1800s. Fish canning is still a major industry, along with shipbuilding and offshore oil drilling. Stavanger is also known for its cathedral, which was begun in 1125.

Western Norway is magnificent, but eastern Norway is easier to live in. Its rolling hills, edging onto mountains, are broken by numerous lakes. Several national parks in this area adjoin national parks in Sweden so that important habitats and wildlife can be more easily preserved. Most of Norway's farms are in this region.

Nord Norge—Land of the Sami

Nord Norge begins near the Arctic Circle and covers almost half of Norway's length. This area includes Finnmark, Norway's largest and northernmost province. The border between Finnmark and the rest of the country marks the place where grain can no longer grow. In other words, Finnmark is very different from the rest of Norway. The northern parts of Finnmark, as well as neighboring Sweden, Finland, and a little bit of Russia, make up Samiland, formerly called "Lapland." The Sami, or Saami, people were once called "Lapps," but they do not like that name because it means "patches of cloth."

Samiland was carved out by a retreating glacier, and it has changed little in the thousands of years that have passed since then. On the west and north—and virtually all in Norway—are mountains and jagged fjords. The remainder of Samiland is mostly a flat plateau—frozen tundra in winter and boggy in summer.

The Land of the Midnight Sun

Northern Norway, ending at North Cape, is often called the "Land of the Midnight Sun." Rough, icy, and stunningly beau-

tiful, the land is lit by sunlight almost twenty-four hours a day
for most of May, June, and July. The penalty for this long summer comes in winter, when the sun cannot be seen above the
horizon during December and most of January. Then this
northern area becomes the "Land of Noontime Darkness."

At almost any time of the year, northern Norway's nighttime sky may be lit with the spectacular aurora borealis, or
northern lights. These curtains and ribbons of colored light in
the sky are most easily seen near the magnetic north pole.

The Nord Norge city of Narvik is a major Arctic port and
gateway to the Lofoten Islands, which are dotted with pic-
turesque fishing villages. The fascinating variety and the
millions of birds that nest in these islands draw bird-watchers
from all over the world. North of the Lofotens are the
Vesterålen Islands, where whales swim off the coasts, especially
off the large island of Andøya.

Hammerfest, located on an island south of North Cape, is Europe's northernmost town. It exists because sealing vessels were drawn to its ice-free harbor. Because of its long winter darkness, Hammerfest became the first town in Norway to have electric streetlights.

National Parks

Norway's first national park was Rondane, north of Lillehammer. Established in 1962, its 222 square miles (575 sq km) consist primarily of barren mountains broken by narrow gorges. Since 1962, seventeen other parks in Norway itself, plus three in the Arctic island group called Svalbard, have been created. They are located in areas where special kinds of forests and wildlife need to be protected.

Øvre Dividal National Park has Norway's four large animals of prey—the brown bear, wolverine, wolf, and lynx. Ormtjernkampen, Norway's smallest national park, contains a small section of eastern Norwegian old-growth spruce forest that has never been logged. Stabbursdalen represents the world's northernmost pine forest.

Norway's Climate

The major factor that makes Norway so livable is the warm waters of the North Atlantic Current, which sweeps the coast. This current is a branch of the Gulf Stream, a huge river of warm water that crosses the Atlantic from the Caribbean Sea. Its warmth makes the country green and lovely. In contrast, Greenland, at about the same latitude as Norway, has a permanent ice sheet covering all but the coastal fringes.

The air above the warm ocean current is also warm, so Norway's coast has warmer weather than would be expected at its northern latitude. The coast has a marine climate, with less temperature difference between winter and summer than regions farther inland. Snow rarely falls along the coast. The inland areas get considerably less precipitation than the coast does, but the snow does not melt as easily.

Near Oslo, the climate is continental, resembling that of mainland Europe, with long, cold winters and dry, warm summers.

Rondane National Park

In January, Oslo's average temperature is 24.2°F (−4.3°C). Its average temperature in July is 61.6°F (16.4°C), but it's often warm enough for sunbathing in the summer.

Amazingly, Samiland, several hundred miles to the north, can be warmer in winter than Oslo. In summer, people can comfortably lie on the sandy beaches of North Cape.

South of the Lofotens, the warm winds of the Atlantic carry a great deal of moisture. As the winds move over Vestlandet, they gradually chill, dropping their moisture. This gives parts of Vestlandet very high precipitation. In fact, parts of coastal Norway have coastal rain forests, similar to those in Oregon and Washington.

Polar Lands

Although North Cape is the northernmost part of Europe, it is not the end of Norwegian land. Far to the north, virtually part of the Arctic ice pack, is an archipelago, or island group, called Svalbard. The main island is Spitsbergen, known for its large coal deposits. Although Svalbard belongs to Norway, several nations have the rights to fish near and mine the islands. More Russians than Norwegians mine the coal on the islands today.

Norwegian territory also includes Jan Mayen Island, which lies east of Greenland. It is the peak of a huge undersea volcano, which was active up to the early eighteenth century. Though inhabited only by people who run a navigation station there, it is important to Norway because of the fishing rights that go along with the island. Iceland and Denmark have often disputed those rights.

In addition to some islands in the Antarctic Ocean, Norway claims a region of Antarctica called Queen Maud Land. This large coastal region lies south of Africa. It was first reached by a Norwegian expedition in 1930 and was named for King Håkon VII's queen.

Amundsen in the Polar Ice

Norwegian explorer Roald Amundsen and his small crew left Norway in June 1903 in a ship that was only 47 feet (14.3 m) long. He was determined to sail across the Arctic Ocean from the North Atlantic to the Pacific in a glacial version of the long-sought "North west Passage." His ship, called the *Gjøa,* was locked in the polar ice for two years as the ice itself slowly moved across the cold sea. Amundsen located the north magnetic pole a considerable distance from the place where it had been found sixty years before, providing the first evidence that Earth's magnetic poles move.

Amundsen later headed for the Antarctic, where he and his men entered a race against Britain's Robert F. Scott, who was also heading for the South Pole. Amundsen was better prepared than Scott and used sled dogs instead of ponies to pull his supplies. Amundsen also had an advantage because he had skied most of his life. On December 14, 1911, Amundsen achieved his goal, becoming the first human to reach the geographic South Pole. He returned to civilization to a tumultuous welcome. Scott and his men died trying to reach the coast.

CHAPTER THREE

The Living Landscape

ONE OF THE LEAST-NOTICED LIVING THINGS in Arctic Norway is one of the most important. It is the lowly lichen, a combination of alga and fungus that spreads across rocky surfaces, even in the most bitter weather. Some lichens are no more than thin layers of color on a rock's surface. Others, especially a type called reindeer moss, are feathery and grow several inches tall, forming a thick blanket on the rock.

When the great glaciers retreated, lichens were the first living things to move into the newly exposed land. In fact, lichens help break up rock, creating soil. Reindeer scrape snow off rocks to find the lichens they depend on for food.

Reindeer moss and other lichens cover the rocks in this pine forest.

Reindeer

The boundaries of Samiland were set long ago by the migrations of the reindeer herds. During the winter, these low-slung relatives of deer—called caribou in North America—roam the Finnmark plateau. The females give birth to calves in May or June. They are in danger for a while from foxes and birds of

Opposite: **A reindeer herd migrating in the spring**

The Sami train reindeer to pull heavy loads.

prey. When the heat of summer draws irritating insects to the flat land, the reindeer head toward the mountains to eat the tender shoots of trees and succulent grasses.

Reindeer differ from other deer in two main ways. The females as well as the males grow antlers, and instead of a single hard hoof on the foot, their hooves are divided so that the foot can spread out on mushy ground. Stocky and very hardy, reindeer have been trained for thousands of years to carry packs and to work in teams pulling loads.

From Norway to the World

One animal for which Norway is known is the Norwegian fjord horse, or *fjording* (above). Accepted as one of the world's oldest breeds, it was probably domesticated in the West Country more than 4,000 years ago and was bred for its specific characteristics at least 2,000 years ago. Fjord horses are fairly small and good-natured. During the reign of King Olav V, the horse was on a Norwegian coin.

Also bred in Norway is a dog called the Norwegian elkhound (right). A medium-sized hunting dog, it was bred perhaps 7,000 years ago for its endurance and its willingness to confront a bear or a charging moose (which the Norwegians called *elg,* or elk). Elkhounds look somewhat like small huskies. They have a light gray coat and a distinctive curled tail.

Less welcome but more widespread is the Norway rat, also known as the brown rat or wharf rat. It is one of the most common rats in cities and farms around the world. Primarily a burrowing, underground animal, it can also swim. It probably spread by traveling aboard ships even in ancient times.

The Big Mammals

The far northern part of Norway has the same kinds of wildlife as the far northern part of North America. Some animals move back and forth between the two areas, traveling around the edges of the ice cap.

Among the first animals to inhabit Norway were the big mammals that had learned to live along the edge of the glaciers, such as reindeer, Arctic foxes, wolves, and wolverines. As the ice retreated northward, these animals followed it, living in the mountains and along the icy shores. Domesticated reindeer graze in Femundsmarka National Park, and a few musk oxen, which were introduced from Greenland, live there for part of the year.

Wolverines are carnivores of the weasel family. Sometimes 3 feet (90 cm) long, these burrowing animals can kill a full-

An Arctic fox

grown reindeer. Wolverines are among the few large Arctic animals that nature has not camouflaged for safety with white fur or feathers. They are so vicious that no other animal dares to attack them.

Large predators such as wolves and bears are rarely seen in Norway today because their forest habitats have been changed by logging. This cutting of trees, however, has increased the number of moose, which feed on the grasses in the open areas.

Beavers were almost extinct in Europe fifty years ago, and only a few breeding colonies of these large rodents still existed in southern Norway. They were successfully protected, however, and Norway has so many beavers today that they are often shipped to other countries to rebuild their beaver populations.

Arctic Camouflage

Some mammals and birds have coloring that protects them in the whiteness of the Arctic. Among the birds of prey that are camouflaged is the snowy owl. A large bird, its white feathers blend in with its snowy surroundings. But when it goes southward where sunlight dapples the forests, it develops bars of dark coloring on the tips of its feathers.

In similar ways, the color of the mountain-dwelling gyrfalcon (left) varies with its surroundings, but unlike the snowy owl, the gyrfalcon takes cover during snowstorms. It burrows into the snow and hibernates while the wind howls. The Arctic gyrfalcon is the world's largest falcon.

The fur of the Arctic fox actually changes color with the season and the environment. It is white in the winter so that it blends with the snow, and it becomes darker, grayish-brown, during the summer. It often scavenges from the leftovers of polar bears.

The Puzzling Lemming

A lemming is a furry rodent about 5 or 6 inches (13 or 15 cm) long. Like all lemmings, the Norway lemming has a population explosion every few years. When the lemming population balloons, the crowded rodents start to move out from their centers of population. Although they are popularly thought to march into the sea to drown, migrating lemmings avoid water unless they can see the shore on the other side. However, they may drown if that shore is farther away than they have the energy to swim. Also, they may fall prey to large hungry fish or birds of prey. Many lemmings die during this grand migration, so the population shrinks. Then the cycle starts all over again.

Birds of Mountain and Coast

The larger birds of regions farther south include grouse, such as the capercaillie, and eagles. However, most of the smaller mountain birds are migratory birds that live there only part of the year. Some come from the coastal areas in summer; others fly north from the Mediterranean Sea. The whimbrel, a long-beaked ground-dwelling bird, flies all the way from Africa to breed in Finnmark.

More permanent residents of the coastal areas include birds that are familiar to seaside dwellers of all northern regions—geese and ducks, cormorants and gulls. Prominent among them is the large sea eagle, or erne, a relative of the American bald eagle.

One of the world's great long-distance fliers comes to Samiland during the summer. The Arctic tern nests along the islands and coasts in the north but heads back to the Antarctic with its young in the fall. It returns again the following spring, having flown incredible distances.

Although the great auk has been extinct since 1844, today's smaller auks are found on the many islands along the northern fjords. The related murres of Bear Island are threatened with extinction because of overfishing in nearby waters. These seabirds require an abundance of fish to survive. Fishing by humans is now being controlled.

The murres of Bear Island

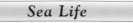
The most important fish of the coastal waters has long been the cod. The cod spawns, or lays its eggs, in the shallow waters around the Lofoten Islands. Cod can be 2 to 3 feet (60 to 90 cm) long and weigh up to 100 pounds (45 kilograms). Norway has exported cod for a thousand years or more, and it is a basic food of the Norwegian people.

Other fish that swim in western waters and can be fished for sport include salmon, trout, and char. Perch, powan, pike, and grayling reach the rivers of eastern Norway from the Baltic Sea.

One of the most plentiful catches off the coast is shrimp. The market in every coastal town carries huge supplies of shrimp each day.

A plantation of young spruce trees next to older ones

A Land of Trees and Flowers

Until about 4,000 years ago, Norway had a warmer climate. The low-lying lands were covered with vast oak forests that provided wood for the earliest human residents. Then the climate cooled. Oak trees, which require warm summers in order to grow, were gradually replaced by other deciduous, or leaf-shedding, trees such as birch and aspen, which are seen widely today.

Soon after the glaciers retreated, the mountains were covered with dense forests of pine and birch. Pine trees stop growing about 31 miles (50 km) south of North Cape. In the cooler climate of recent centuries, the blue spruce tree—appropriately called the Norway spruce—has taken over much of the pine land.

On the mountainsides, the trees change according to elevation. The lower slopes are covered with conifers, especially spruce. Above the conifers is a belt of birch, aspen, and mountain ash. Higher yet, just below the tree line, may be some fairly low-growing willow and dwarf birch. The tree line is about 4,000 feet (1,200 m) in the south but only about half that high in the far north. The treeless mountaintops are dotted with lakes and covered with low-growing plants and tiny wildflowers. Most of Dovrefjell National Park is above the tree line and consists of open moorland, which is often marshy.

Wildflowers in Samiland

Samiland's summer is very short, but plants take advantage of the extra daylight to grow quickly, creating a wondrous display of wildflowers where it seems nothing should grow. In the north, the wildflowers tend to be plants that spread from Siberia. The Dovre and Jotunheim Mountains in the south and some areas farther north grow about thirty species of mountain plants that came from Canada and Greenland. No one is sure how the plants got there or why they don't spread elsewhere in the mountains of Europe.

A baby seal from the north

The coastal islands and fjords swarm with seals of various kinds. When the number of fish in the coastal waters seriously decreased, the number of seals dropped, too. But protection of the fishing waters and of the seals has increased their populations once again.

Norway has always been a whaling nation. In agreement with the Convention on International Trade in Endangered Species, and following a ban by the International Whaling

Commission, it stopped commercial whaling in 1985. Because whaling was so important to its economy, though, Norway started whaling again in 1992.

Norway and several other nations were foresighted enough in the 1960s to introduce measures to preserve polar bears, most of which are found in the Svalbard Islands. Norway entirely outlawed hunting these great bears. Today, these marvelous but dangerous animals are out of danger.

A polar bear on the coast of Spitsbergen about to go swimming

Determined to Be Free

As THE GREAT GLACIERS RETREATED, LIVING THINGS— including humans—moved northward, especially along the seacoast. The earliest Norwegians probably arrived from Central Asia about 10,000 years ago. They fished and moved through the area now called Finnmark, where they probably evolved into the Sami people.

A few thousand years later, more people moved north into Norway, this time from Germany. Tools and other items used by these people have been found in central and southern Norway. They evolved into the people we call Norwegians.

Starting about 6,000 years ago, the Norwegians rowed boats across the Skagerrak to the mainland of Europe, where they traded for metals they could not find at home. By about 1500 B.C., agriculture had become the main occupation in southern Norway, while the rest of the people depended on fishing and hunting.

The Viking Era

In A.D. 793, Scandinavian seamen—warriors who came to be known as Vikings—put together their sailing skills, their supplies of iron for weapons, their need for new land, and their spirit of adventure, and gave their name to an era. For almost

300 years, these Scandinavian wayfarers raided Europe, plundering treasure houses and taking slaves. They sailed their marvelous ships up the rivers of Russia, the European continent, the British Isles, and even into the Mediterranean Sea.

But why? There were probably many reasons. One of the most important was that there was a population explosion in Scandinavia. Norway has very little farmland. If there were too many sons in a family, there was not enough land for each son to have a farm. Younger sons had to hunt for other land.

As far as the rest of the European world was concerned, the era began at the island of Lindisfarne, off the coast of England in the North Sea. The monks who lived there were terrified when the high-prowed Viking ships landed on the beaches of their island. The Vikings plundered the monastery and returned home with gold and other treasures. Their success showed other Scandinavians an easy way to obtain wealth.

A Norse Sea-King

The Norwegian Vikings also wanted the land in the places they invaded, hoping to settle. They occupied the Orkney and Shetlands Islands off the northern coast of Scotland. They continued on around Scotland and took the Hebrides Islands off the western coast, and then, in 831, they moved to Ireland.

In Ireland, many of the strongly Christian people now called Celts fought fiercely, but the Vikings stayed long enough for the military camp and trading center they built up to become the city of Dublin. When the Danes arrived a few years later, the Norwegians and the Danes fought for control of Ireland. In 853, Olav, a Norwegian warlord, won. He and his Vikings ruled Ireland until 871.

A Norse Raid under Olaf

Viking Ships

Boats built by the ancient Scandinavians always had to be rowed by powerful men. But the Vikings added a new idea to their boats—sails. They built their longboats with a shallow draft that allowed them to sail up shallow rivers, taking inland villages by surprise. The dragon's head on the ship's prow was to forestall evil.

The Viking longboats had open decks, with no protection from storms or waves. The sailors often spent entire journeys wet and cold. Only when traveling along a coast could they stop and build a fire on the shore. The Vikings used a primitive compass of naturally magnetic lodestone to find their way across wide oceans.

In 1880, an ancient burial mound was unearthed at Gokstad in southeastern Norway. It contained many wonderful treasures, including an almost perfectly preserved Viking ship. A man named Magnus Andersen saw the ship and set out to prove that ancient Norwegians had visited North America long before Columbus.

Andersen raised the money to have a replica of the ship built. With twelve willing sailors at the oars, he sailed from Bergen to Canada in twenty-eight days. When the ship pulled into the harbor at Chicago, Illinois, to visit the 1893 Columbian Exposition, the new Gokstad ship was the most popular exhibit at the World's Fair.

Leif the Lucky

Leif Eriksson was one of the sons of Erik the Red, leader of the Viking colony that settled Greenland in the 900s. But Leif was willing to explore even farther. Returning from a trip to Norway, Eriksson bypassed Greenland and sailed to the North American continent, probably the area now known as Nova Scotia. He called it Vinland, thinking of the wine that could be made from the many grapevines he saw. Small Viking settlements were soon established in eastern Canada, but they did not last long. In the 1960s, the remains of a settlement thought to date from the Viking era were found in Newfoundland.

On to Iceland and Greenland

A.D. 874—another adventure begins. Some Norwegian Vikings, still in search of good land, bypass Ireland. After bravely sailing the better part of 700 miles (1,127 km), they reach a large island that has fjords and mountains like their native Norway. This island we now call Iceland was quite green and fertile, kept warm by the Gulf Stream and the land's natural hot springs.

By 930, Iceland was a nation, the Icelandic Commonwealth, with a legislature called the Althing. Later settlers were unable to find usable land in this island of volcanoes so they sailed farther west and founded settlements on Greenland. And from Greenland, Vikings became the first Europeans to reach the North American continent.

A Bard Reciting to Northmen

ARCTIC OCEAN

Arctic Circle

ICELAND   NORWAY

Finns

ATLANTIC
OCEAN   SWEDEN

RUSSIA

North   DENMARK   Balts
Sea

Poles

FRANKISH   Slovaks
KINGDOMS   Magyars

Sicily

AFRICA   Mediterranean Sea

Viking Raids 800–1035

■ Norwegian settlements   ■ Swedish settlements
▨ Empire of Canute 1035   ■ Danish settlements
— Norwegian raids

Saga of the Kings

Much of what we know about the Viking era comes from writings preserved in Iceland, especially those by Snorri Sturluson. One of his books, called the *Heimskringla (Saga of the Kings),* relates the exploits of Norwegian chieftains and kings. In some cases, Sturluson used his own imagination. In others, he recorded the poetry of the bards who told the tales of the great leaders.

The first kings of Norway to leave historical proof of their existence were two half-brothers, Olav and Halvdan, who lived in the mid-800s. Olav, who was known as a good and brave king, was buried in a huge mound along with his ship. That ship was found centuries later by archaeologists. Halvdan, called Halvdan the Svart (Black), was the founder of a line of Norwegian kings.

Halvdan's son, Harald, became king when he was only ten years old. According to legend, he brought the many small kingdoms of Norway into one kingdom in the 800s to win a bride. The beautiful Gyda had refused to marry him until he unified Norway.

During the years that Harald was working to unify the country, he vowed never to cut his hair until the task was done. He went down in history as Harald Hårfager (Fairhair). Even though Harald acquired a number of other wives while working on Gyda's challenge, he eventually married her. However, he later divorced them all so that he could marry a Danish princess. With so many wives, Harald had many sons. After unifying Norway, he broke it up again by giving pieces of the country to each son.

Rollo, Duke of Normandy by Gianni Dagli Orti

Norsemen Become Normans

Most of the Vikings attacking France were Danes, but their leader was probably a Norwegian. He was called Rolf by the Norwegians and Rollo by the French. By the year 911, they had made such nuisances of themselves that the French king agreed to give Rollo a large section of land around the mouth of the Seine River. Rollo and his men established a settlement called Normandy, after the Norsemen.

By 1066, when the Norsemen, or Normans, from France conquered England, the Viking era was ending, but their legacy lived on. The Scandinavian warriors had explored and extended the known world. They had built cities and traded with distant peoples. They had changed the map of western Europe.

From Pagan to Christian

The Vikings believed in many gods, especially Odin and Thor, but many Vikings who settled in Christian countries became Christians. Christianity was brought to Norway about A.D. 995 by Olav Tryggvason, who became King Olav I. A great-grandson of Harald Fairhair, Olav (also spelled Olaf) had been raised in Russia, where he trained to become both a Viking warrior and a Christian. He tried to force his religion on his people, but the people paid little attention.

A few years later, Olav II, who was also baptized outside Norway, was more successful in turning his people to Christianity. His major success, however, occurred after his death in battle, when he was declared a saint and became Norway's patron saint, Olav the Holy or Saint Olav.

These first kings were significant, but they didn't have total control over the country. Several times in the next few centuries, two or even more kings ruled at the same time in different places. Starting in about 1130, there was a long period of civil war between two far-reaching families. At the end of the fighting, about 1217, Håkon Håkonsson was in control of a single unified nation. He was crowned King Håkon IV.

Ruling Merchants

In about 1300, Håkon V began trading with merchants from northern Germany. The big German merchant cities had combined themselves into an organization called the Hanseatic League. (A *hansa* was a company of merchants.) They took advantage of a catastrophe—the plague called the Black Death.

The Black Death spread from southern Europe into Norway starting in about 1349. It wiped out perhaps half of Norway's people. The surviving traders of the Hanseatic League took control of some parts of Norway, especially around Bergen. For centuries, the fishers of the coasts had to deal with the league officials in order to sell their catch. However, the league took charge of selling the fish abroad, and much of coastal Norway prospered.

Union with Denmark

In 1363, Norwegian King Håkon VI, son of the Swedish king, married Margrethe, daughter of the Danish king. All the chips were in place for these three Scandinavian nations to become one. And in 1397, Margrethe organized the Union of Kalmar, by which her son would become the first ruler of a unified Scandinavia.

The three countries never did become one, however, and the Union of Kalmar was finally dissolved in 1523. Sweden

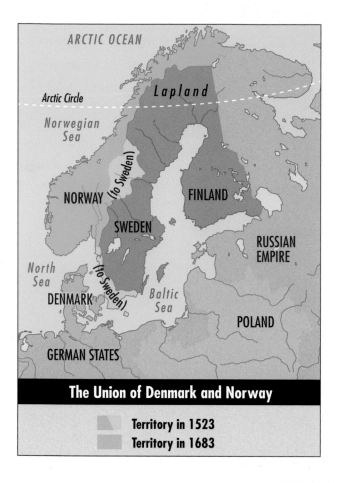

ARCTIC OCEAN

Arctic Circle

Norwegian Sea

Lapland

NORWAY (to Sweden)

FINLAND

SWEDEN

RUSSIAN EMPIRE

North Sea

(to Sweden)

Baltic Sea

DENMARK

POLAND

GERMAN STATES

The Union of Denmark and Norway

Territory in 1523
Territory in 1683

managed to break free and set its own course, but Norway remained tied to Denmark for another three centuries. The dual kingdom of Denmark-Norway was created, with Christian III as king. Norway's national council was eliminated. Norway was regarded by the Danes as a mere province of Denmark.

It's amazing that Norway kept its own culture after 300 years as part of Denmark. The Danes allowed Norway to grow and develop, primarily because its people were useful to Denmark as seafarers who came to know and understand the wider world. However, nearly all the wealth generated in Norway made its way to Denmark, and the Norwegians became increasingly bitter.

Sweden Wins the Prize

A new civil war might have started if another war had not affected Denmark-Norway first. French emperor Napoléon Bonaparte's war to take over Europe led to a blockade across the Skagerrak. By 1807, Norway was cut off from Denmark. Denmark itself was an ally of Napoléon's, which meant that Norway had to side with Napoléon against the British. When Napoléon was defeated, Sweden, which fought on the side of the British, claimed Norway as its prize. In January 1814, Norway was handed over to Sweden.

Being a prize wasn't all bad, however. In giving Norway to Sweden, Denmark insisted that Norway have the right to run itself. In addition, the Danish governor of Norway, Prince Christian Frederik, provoked a revolt by the Norwegians, hoping that he might end up the king of a new nation. He urged Norwegian officials to go ahead and write their own constitution. They met at Eidsvoll to put their vision of an independent country in a constitution.

When the Norwegians signed their Constitution, Sweden sent troops into Norway. Unprepared for such a move, the Norwegians had to give in. King Christian Frederik gave up his throne, and the Swedish king became the new king of Norway. Sweden was quite gracious, however, and agreed that the Norwegians could—with a few minor changes—live by the Constitution they had written at Eidsvoll.

Syttende Mai

In 1814, when the union with Denmark was dissolved, 112 representatives of the Norwegian people met at Eidsvoll, north of Oslo, and wrote a constitution for what they hoped would become an independent country. They signed it on May 17, 1814. That date is now a Norwegian holiday, *Syttende Mai* (May Seventeenth). Also called Constitution Day, Syttende Mai is celebrated around the world wherever Norwegians gather.

Making the Storting

In the years following 1814, the people continually found themselves at odds with the Swedish king and his representatives, who often took actions without consulting the Norwegian legislature, called the Storting. But according to the Norwegian Constitution, the Storting met only every third year. Thus it really had no power. By 1869, people were tired of not being consulted. They changed the Constitution so that the Storting had to meet every year.

In 1884, after the Storting tried to impeach, or remove from office, one minister, an agreement was reached. Under this agreement, the cabinet of the king's ministers was no longer appointed by the Swedish king. Instead, the ministers were appointed from among the ranks of people elected to the Norwegian Storting. This is why, even though the Storting existed long before, 1884 is often regarded as its real starting date.

An Independent Nation

As the end of the nineteenth century approached, Norwegians increasingly demanded the separation of Norway from Sweden. Protests came to a head on June 7, 1905, when the Storting voted to set up embassies and consular offices representing Norway abroad. The Swedish king refused to agree, insisting that Norway, as a part of Sweden, did not have the right to represent itself abroad. On August 13, 1905, Norwegians voted on whether to remain with Sweden or become independent. Of the 368,208 people who voted, only 184 chose to remain part of Sweden.

Sweden did not protest very hard at losing Norway. A new nation was born, based on a constitution that had been written almost a hundred years before.

World War I and Its Aftermath

Almost the first crisis to confront Norway was international—the advent of World War I in 1914. Norwegians chose to remain neutral and learn to be an independent nation. However, because Norway's merchant ships traveled all over the world, the country suffered great losses in shipping. Also, the people went hungry when the fighting interfered with their food imports.

Norway's serious economic troubles continued until the mid-1920s. The nation had only just begun to recover when the worldwide troubles of the Great Depression started in about 1930. Fortunately, Norway was already well on its way to becoming a strong industrial nation.

In Germany, the Depression—along with the aftereffects of World War I, which Germany lost—made life very difficult. When Adolf Hitler and his National Socialist (Nazi) Party promised to make life better, the

Adolf Hitler inspects his personal guard.

German people elected Hitler chancellor of Germany. They didn't know that Hitler would soon become a dictator and lead Germany into another terrible war—one that would spread across the whole world.

As World War II approached in the late 1930s, Norway had an active army of only about 7,000 men—and those men had never even learned field maneuvers. The navy was no better—its ships had not left port since 1918.

German tanks in Oslo during World War II

War Again

World War II began in September 1939, when Nazi troops invaded Poland. Britain and France, which were committed to protecting Poland, declared war against Germany. Norway wanted to be neutral, but the Nazis would not allow that. On April 8, 1940, Nazi ships sailed through the large fjords of southern Norway and into the big ports of Oslo, Stavanger, and Bergen.

Vidkun Quisling

Troops from Germany arrived by ship and by air, but not before Norway's royal family and the leaders of the government managed to escape from Oslo. They set up a new government in Tromsø, but no one was in charge in the capital. Into the limelight marched a strange man whose name came to mean "traitor"—Vidkun Quisling.

On the evening of April 9, Quisling announced to the Norwegian people that he had every right to form a new gov-

Elverum was destroyed by German bombs.

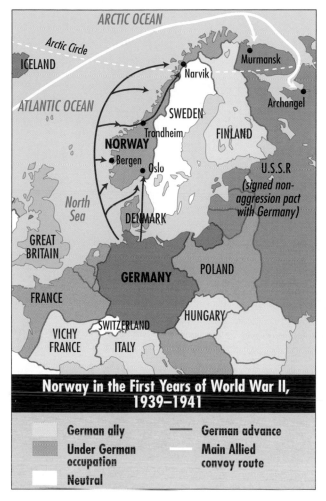
Norway in the First Years of World War II, 1939–1941

German ally — German advance
Under German occupation — Main Allied convoy route
Neutral

ernment because the government had abandoned Oslo. He said the people should not oppose the Nazis—they should, in fact, collaborate with, or help, them. Some Norwegians were drawn to Quisling's government and collaborated with the Nazis throughout the war. But most people did what they could to resist.

King Happy Said "No!"

Because King Håkon VII always seemed to be smiling, he was called King Happy by the Norwegian people. But his smile disappeared when, on April 10, 1940, Vidkun Quisling demanded that the king officially name Quisling's political party as the government and make Quisling the prime minister. King Håkon refused. "No!" he said. When the Storting, forced by the Nazis, demanded that he abdicate, or give up the throne, again Håkon said "No!" Instead, he and the government fled to Britain and led the Norwegian resistance from there.

Norwegians were searched
by German soldiers after
being captured.

Nazi troops arrived in force and occupied Norway. The first months of occupation were very confusing. Most people didn't know what to do or how to act. But Quisling knew what he wanted. He wanted to make it appear as if the Norwegians were willing to accept the occupation, and even eager to help Germany dominate Europe.

Individually and in groups, many Norwegians began to resist doing the things the Hitler-controlled government wanted done. Resistance might be as simple as failing to catch fish that enemy troops needed to eat, or as involved and dangerous as sabotaging a railway. Workers in factories often carried out what was called "silent sabotage"—working slowly so that products did not get made in the numbers Germany needed. But resistance was dangerous, too. The Nazi troops often executed people who resisted.

In 1942, Hitler named Quisling premier, or "minister president," of Norway. When Quisling tried to insist that all children from the age of nine up participate in Nazi training programs, thousands of teachers and parents protested. More than a thousand teachers were arrested, and some were shipped off to work camps. Churches also backed the protest, with more than 4,000 ministers resigning their positions. Eventually, the Quisling government canceled the order for young people to go into training. News of the success of this widespread resistance leaked to the world, and people everywhere were awestruck at little Norway's defying the powerful Nazis.

U.S. president Franklin Delano Roosevelt said in a speech, "If there is anyone who doubts the democratic will to win . . . let him look to Norway. He will find in Norway, at once conquered and unconquerable, the answer to his questioning."

The End

Toward the end of the war, the Germans were losing the fight for Europe. Rather than be forced to join the German troops in a last-ditch effort to win the war, thousands of young Norwegians left home in the night and hid in the dense forests. Many Norwegians went hungry in order to secretly send their food to the "lads in the forests."

In the final weeks of the war, troops from the Soviet Union forced Nazi soldiers to retreat through Finland into Norway. The Nazis burned or blew up every town, farm, machine, and factory along the way, trying to prevent anything useful reaching the hands of the oncoming Soviet troops. Towns and villages in northern Norway were wiped out, and the Nazis forced more than 50,000 Sami and other Norwegians southward with them.

Sabotage by Ski

The Norsk Hydro plant in Telemark was the only place in the world where "heavy water" was manufactured. Heavy water is a form of water that contains hydrogen atoms different from those in most water. The Nazis wanted to use the heavy water to make an atomic bomb. Before the Nazis could take the heavy-water supplies, a few brave Norwegians skied along an icy mountain path so dangerous that the Germans were certain it could not be used. These resistance fighters penetrated the Norsk Hydro plant and blew it up, along with the precious supplies of heavy water. This story was later told in the movie *The Heroes of Telemark*.

When Norwegians learned from their contacts in Britain that the war was almost over, they made plans for taking control of their own country again. Nazi troops all over Europe surrendered, and on May 8, 1945, Norwegian flags, long tucked away, flew from every house. Five years of occupation by the enemy had ended. When the legitimate government returned, about 19,000 Norwegians were sent to prison for collaborating with the enemy during the war. Twenty-four people, including Vidkun Quisling, were executed.

Joining Nations

After World War II, the Norwegian people realized that they could no longer remain neutral if they wanted to remain free and independent. They joined the United Nations (UN) when it was formed in 1945 and the North Atlantic Treaty Organization (NATO) when it was organized in 1949. NATO's mission was to unify the armed forces of the countries that opposed the might of the Soviet Union, which had a huge military force.

The Nordic Council, formed in 1952, includes the five Scandinavian nations of Norway, Sweden, Denmark, Finland, and Iceland. A citizen of one is, in effect, a citizen of all five. Individuals can move freely among these nations, traveling without passports, and they can work in any one of them. The countries also combine their efforts in communication and transportation.

Soon after the Nordic Council was formed, most European nations began talking about having a similar organization to eliminate barriers among European countries. Initially called the Common Market, the organization's name was later changed to the European Union (EU). The EU voted in 1994 to admit Norway, but the citizens of a nation must approve its being a member. The Norwegian people voted against EU membership 52.2 percent to 47.8 percent.

There were two main reasons for the vote against membership in the EU. First, Norway had been an independent country for less than a century, so the people didn't want once again to turn over important decisions to outsiders. And, second, Norway has the economic strength, because of its natural resources, to remain independent.

Building for the Future

Following the rebuilding of its cities and industries after World War II, Norway began to grow economically and has continued to thrive. At the same time, the social benefits of that growth were built into the economy, so citizens are guaranteed security.

Norway has not let its military forces get weak again, as it did after World War I. The country plays an important role in UN peacekeeping operations around the world. It has also been involved in the continuing negotiations between Israel and the Palestinians to solve the Middle East peace crisis. Norway has also welcomed refugees from around the world.

Tings
and Towns

EARLY IN NORWAY'S HISTORY, THE PEOPLE BEGAN TO GATHER in assemblies to decide issues that involved the whole community. Such an assembly was called a *ting*. A higher-level assembly, representing a number of tings, was the *lagting*. The lagting could approve—or ratify—laws passed by the tings. It also could communicate directly with the king. Some of the places where the lagting met became the first towns in Norway. Trondheim, for instance, was organized in A.D. 997 and is the oldest city.

Building a Constitution and a Monarchy

Because Denmark ruled them until 1814, Norwegians had little opportunity for several centuries to build democratic legislative assemblies. Then, the Danish crown prince, Christian Frederik, called a meeting. He hoped that if he could separate Norway from Sweden, he could be Norway's king. Instead, the men at the meeting created a constitution that made Norway a constitutional monarchy. They would choose the king instead of the king choosing them.

Because Norway is a constitutional monarchy, the king, whose position is inherited, has no power on his own to make decisions affecting the country. He can act only through the

Norway's royal family

government, called the King-in-Council. The State Council, or *Statsråd*, acts for the monarch. It consists of the prime minister and at least seven other people.

When Harald V, grandson of Håkon VII, became king in 1991, Norway had a queen for the first time in more than fifty years. She is a commoner named Sonja. Their son, the heir to the throne, is Crown Prince Håkon, born in 1973. His sister, Princess Martha Louise, is two years older.

Until recently, Norway had a law that only a male born to a king could inherit the throne. The Constitution was changed in 1990 so that a woman can rule, but it was decided at the time that the change would affect only women born after 1990. Princess Martha Louise can become queen only if young Håkon, the crown prince, dies before having children of his own.

Electing a King

Several months after choosing independence from Sweden in August 1905, the people voted again. This time they decided that although the nation would be a democracy, they wanted to have a monarch. The Norwegians asked Crown Prince Carl of Denmark to become their new king.

Harking back to Viking days, Prince Carl took the name of Håkon VII. It was more than 500 years since Håkon VI had reigned. Håkon VII's wife was Princess Maud, daughter of King Edward VII of England. They are shown here with their son, Prince Olaf. Håkon reigned through two world wars, from 1905 to 1957.

Norway's National Anthem

Bjørnstjerne Bjørnson (right), a Nobel Prize–winning poet, dramatist, and politician, wrote the Norwegian national anthem, *"Ja, vi elsker dette landet ("Yes, We Love This Land")*, which was officially adopted in 1864 on the fiftieth anniversary of the creation of the Constitution. The music was written by Bjørnson's young cousin Rikard Nordråk.

Yes, we love with fond devotion
this land of ours that looms
rugged, storm-scarred o'er this ocean,
with her thousand homes.
Love her in our love recalling
those who gave us birth,
and old tales which night in falling
brings as dreams to earth,
And old tales which night in falling
brings as dreams as dreams to earth.

Norsemen what-so-e'er thy station
thank thy God whose power
willed and wrought the land's salvation
in her darkest hour.
All our mothers sought in weeping
and our sires in fight
God has fashioned in his keeping
till we gained our right.
God has fashioned in his keeping
till we gained we gained our right.

Today's Storting

Until 1989, the Storting had 157 members, but eight were added to represent political parties that are too small to elect members on their own. The Storting today has 165 members who are elected for four years at a time.

Although the Storting is only one legislative house, it has two divisions. The members divide themselves into a small upper house, called the Lagting, while the larger group forms the lower house—the *Odelsting*. A bill must be approved by the Odelsting before it is sent to the Lagting.

The Norwegian Parliament in session

**National Government
of Norway**

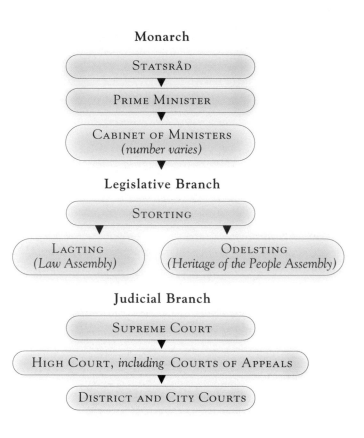

Monarch

STATSRÅD

PRIME MINISTER

CABINET OF MINISTERS
(number varies)

Legislative Branch

STORTING

LAGTING
(Law Assembly)

ODELSTING
(Heritage of the People Assembly)

Judicial Branch

SUPREME COURT

HIGH COURT, *including* COURTS OF APPEALS

DISTRICT AND CITY COURTS

The Storting names the prime minister as well as the government ministers who form the cabinet. They can come from inside the legislature—in which case they are no longer members of the Storting—or from outside. The ministers and the Storting must function together until a new election is held, which happens every four years.

Local Government

The 1814 constitution gave just as much power to the local governments as it did to the national government. Norway is

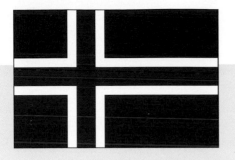

The Norwegian Flag

For centuries, as a minority partner in Denmark-Norway, Norway had no flag of its own. It used the Danish flag, which is red with a white cross on it. In 1814, when Norway's constitution was written, the Storting voted to continue using that flag but to add a blue cross inside the white one. The U.S., British, and French flags display these colors, so red, white, and blue are regarded by Norwegians as the "colors of freedom."

During the years of Swedish rule, the red-white-and-blue Norwegian flag was positioned in the upper-left corner of the Swedish flag, which is blue and yellow. This made a very "busy" flag that Norwegians often sneered at, calling it "herring salad." As soon as Norway became independent in 1905, the red-white-and-blue flag was flown again.

Counties (Fylker)

1	Akershus	11	Oslo
2	Aust-Agder	12	Østfold
3	Buskerud	13	Rogaland
4	Finnmark	14	Sogn og Fjordane
5	Hedmark	15	Sør-Trøndelag
6	Hordaland	16	Telemark
7	Møre og Romsdal	17	Troms
8	Nordland	18	Vest-Agder
9	Nord-Trøndelag	19	Vestfold
10	Oppland		

divided into nineteen provinces, or counties, called *fylker*. The largest fylke in area is Finnmark in the far north, which is where the Sami live, but it is the smallest in population. The smallest fylke in area is Oslo, which has the largest population.

There are also about 435 municipalities. (Oslo is both a province and a municipality.) Only 10 of the 435 municipalities have populations of 50,000 or more.

The Supreme Court building

Norway has had a law code since about 1270, when King Magnus the Lawmender compiled regional codes into a national code. Today's judicial system starts with local, lower courts. There are district courts (*Herredsrett*) and city courts (*Byrett*). Both civil and criminal cases may be sent to a high court, the *Lagmannsrett*. The high court also includes six courts of appeal where cases may be sent if one party or the other wants to fight a lower-court decision. Finally, at the top is the nation's Supreme Court, or *Høyesterett*. The Supreme Court has eighteen judges. Judges at all levels are recommended by an advisory body and appointed by the king.

Before a civil, or noncriminal, case reaches a full-fledged court action, a conciliation board, made up of people in the community, often settles it first. This board tries to get the people involved to reach an agreement without the time and expense of going to court.

Norway has forty-eight police districts that oversee the work of local police departments. In addition, there are sev-

Norwegian soldiers standing in front of a tank

eral national policing bodies, such as the National Bureau of Crime Investigation. The maximum time a criminal may serve in prison is twenty-one years. There is no death penalty.

Norway's military plays an important role in the North Atlantic Treaty Organization. Every male between ages nineteen and forty-four is expected to train and serve in the army, navy, or air force and on reserve, if needed.

Taxes and Social Benefits

Norway is most often described as a social democratic welfare state. This means that it places a high value on the welfare—

Oslo: Did You Know This?

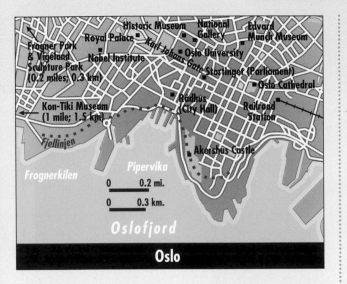

Oslo was founded by King Harold Hårdråde in about 1050, but it did not become the capital of Norway until 1299. It is located at the head of the Oslofjord, which knifes northward from the Skagerrak, the strait between Norway and Denmark. Oslo lies in a particularly beautiful setting, with water along one side and mountains creating a bowl on the others. The city itself spreads up the mountainsides.

Very little in Oslo dates from before 1624, when half of the city's population died of the terrible plague called the Black Death and the city was then was destroyed by fire. The king decreed that the city must never burn down again, and so all buildings had to be constructed of stone or brick.

Unlike many cities, Oslo today does not have a skyline of towering buildings that makes people ooh and ahh, but it does have a bustling, thriving downtown. Oslo's main street is Karl Johans Gate (opposite page), named for the Swedish king who was in power when Sweden took over Norway. The central railway station is located at one end, and the Royal Palace (*Slottet*) is at the other. The old buildings of the University of Oslo, the National Gallery, and the Historical Museum stand on this street, as does the Storting. A medieval castle and fortress called the Akershus Slott lies on a small peninsula in central Oslo. During World War II, German forces were headquartered there, and the fortress contains a museum dedicated to the Norwegian resistance.

Streetcars and subways take people in just about any direction. People can fish, swim, ski, ski jump, skate, hike, and picnic—as well as, of course, work and live—in Oslo. There are hundreds of miles of hiking trails and more than 300 lakes within the city limits.

One reason that Oslo has remained so livable is that it is not given over entirely to cars. City officials firmly believe that the public transportation system should work for the almost 500,000 people who live there. If buses or trains are more than twenty minutes late, the system pays taxi fares to send the passengers home.

the physical, social, educational, and economic health—of individual citizens. It is important to Norwegians that everyone be approximately equal in social and economic standing.

If people cannot get jobs, they still receive a salary. Workers have excellent retirement benefits, and all health-care and education costs are paid for by the government. In order to grant all citizens so many benefits, taxes in Norway are among the highest in the world. Most people are satisfied with the system though, because they never have to worry about being unemployed or how they will pay for health care or old age.

Many voters call for lower taxes, but they also want to keep all the benefits. No one has figured out how to have it both ways.

The Prize for Peace

Alfred Nobel, a Swedish chemist and business-man who invented dynamite as a safe way of handling explosives, died a wealthy man in 1896. In his will, he established a series of prizes for progress in the sciences. They are awarded in Sweden. Nobel also left money to award a prize for achievements in working toward peace. He left the decisions regarding the Nobel Peace Prize to Norway, though no one knows why.

The first Norwegian to be awarded the presti-gious Nobel Peace Prize was Christian Lange, in 1921. He was one of the world's leading peace advocates. The following year, Arctic explorer Fridtjof Nansen received the award. He was a major influence in organizing huge programs to return World War I refugees and prisoners of war to their own lands and to help feed the starving Russians.

Women in Norway

Women in Norway gained control over their own wealth in the 1890s and, at about the same time, acquired the right to vote in local elections. They were allowed to vote in the national Storting elections in 1913. Two years before that, however, in 1911, a schoolteacher named Anna Rogstadt became the first woman elected to the Storting.

Since the 1970s, Norwegian women have worked to take their place in the country's government, at the local, county, and national level. Prime Minister Gro Harlem Brundtland had almost as many women as men in her cabinet. In recent years, approximately half of all cabinet ministers have been women. Sweden and then Norway lead the world in the number of women in their national parliaments.

Wealth from the Sea

Even in Viking times, Norwegians sold their fish and their timber—sometimes by building boats—to other countries. These activities are still important in Norway's economy.

Norway got a later start on the Industrial Revolution than most countries. The first true industries, which were textile mills and paper-pulp plants, started in the 1840s.

Norway was already on its way to a secure industrial future in the 1960s when petroleum and natural gas deposits were found under the North Sea. These deposits are shared by Britain and Norway. Norwegians know that these resources will not last very long, so they are taking advantage of them to build new industries that will provide continuing security.

Norwegian farmland in autumn

Agriculture

Norway has very little agricultural land. Most of the land is mountainous, and regular crops cannot easily be grown because of the difficulty of using machinery on mountainsides. Fruit trees, which do not require level ground, are important crops.

Most farms are quite small and are still in the hands of individual farmers. On those open

fields, the main crops are grains. Barley is the most important crop, followed by potatoes, oats, wheat, and rye. These crops are used at home, and Norwegians must import almost all their other food.

Norway at Sea

All ships that travel the seas must be registered with a country, but it doesn't need to be the country from which the ship actually comes. Many ships are registered in other countries because of those countries' tax structures or their rules. The Norwegian International Ship Registry, formed in 1987, is one of the largest registries in the world.

Ships of Norwegian registry rarely dock in Norway. They wander the world carrying goods from port to port. Their sailors, however, live under the rules established for Norwegian ships.

The Norwegian Cruise Line is one of the great passenger cruise lines of the world. It is building four new ships carrying as many as 2,000 passengers each.

Steel-making plants
in Mo-i-Rana

Natural Resources

Norway has made its business out of its natural resources, but it doesn't take them lightly. The nation is rich in forests, and wood-processing is still a major industry.

Petroleum and natural gas are Norway's major mineral resources. It also mines iron, titanium, copper, zinc, and lead. The Svalbard Islands have hard-coal mines.

Narvik is an iron-ore shipping center. Much of the ore collected there is shipped to Mo-i-Rana, a major steel-making town. This town's strange name tells you it is the town of Mo on the Rana River. It is located almost at the Arctic Circle.

The main item of Norwegian trade from Viking times until recently has been dried fish. Nowadays, the fish are more likely to be frozen or canned. Herring, cod,

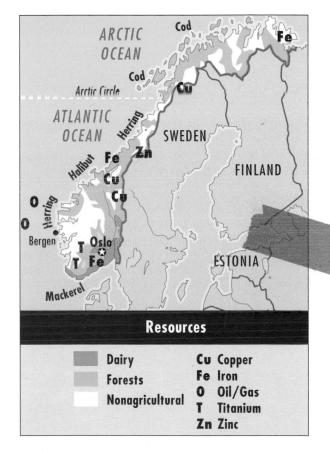

Resources

Dairy	**Cu** Copper
Forests	**Fe** Iron
Nonagricultural	**O** Oil/Gas
	T Titanium
	Zn Zinc

Iron Miners at Risk

Kirkenes is an iron-ore town, as well as the last stop on the steamer from Bergen. During World War II, the Nazis made slaves of the people, forcing them to work in the area's iron mines. When the town was being bombed to force out the Nazi troops, the residents hid in railway tunnels for three weeks, often without food.

What Norway Grows, Makes, and Mines

Agriculture (1996)

Barley	645,000 metric tons
Potatoes	400,000 metric tons
Oats	380,000 metric tons

Manufacturing (1994; value added in kroner)

Machinery and equipment	37,194,000,000
Paper and paper products	19,748,000,000
Food products	17,375,000,000

Mining (1996)

Iron ore	1,554,599 metric tons
Ilmenite-titanium	758,711 metric tons
Copper	31,736 metric tons

and mackerel are the most important catches. Millions of tons of sardines go through the canning plants at Stavanger, known as the "sardine capital of the world."

Tromsø was the center of the whaling industry until the International Whaling Commission banned whaling in 1985 so that whale populations would have a chance to increase again. In 1992, Norwegian whalers started hunting the minke whale again. This may have helped some coastal communities, but it has angered conservationists.

In the north, along the coast, hunting seals for fur and blubber is a big business, which the Norwegian government regulates carefully. However, Norwegians often come into conflict with animal rights and environmental activists.

A fishmonger in Bergen

Under the North Sea

Oil was discovered under the North Sea in 1969. This bonanza is shared by Norway and the United Kingdom. Norway has become one of the main oil-exporting nations of the world.

The first oil field discovered was given the name Ekofisk. It is located about halfway between Norway and England. The other fields in the area have been combined under the name Ekofisk District. The petroleum taken from it is sent by pipeline to refineries in England.

Opposite: **Fishing sheds on the Lofoten Islands**

The Kroner

The basic unit of currency in Norway is the *krone,* which means "crown." The plural is *kroner.* One krone is made up of 100 *øre.* Coins of 10 and 50 øres and of 1, 5, and 10 kroner are issued, and notes come in denominations of 50, 100, 200, 500, and 1,000 kroner.

During the reign of Håkon VII, Norwegian coins had a hole in the center, with four crowns spaced around the hole, forming a cross. In a new series of coins introduced since Harald V became king, the hole appears again, in the 5 kroner coin.

The fact that the oil refining is not done in Norway has helped the country preserve its environment. In addition, Norway has taken extreme care in its offshore drilling and pumping. The only blowout in which oil escaped into the North Sea occurred in April 1977.

Norway's population of more than 4,400,000 is too small for the country to produce most of the goods they need, so Norway depends on its ability to trade with other countries. However, the nation has been very fortunate in having oil and natural gas to export. It can spend its export revenue to bring in the imported products it needs.

Norway depends heavily on hydroelectric power generated by dams on the fjords and rivers. As a result, when there is a period of little rainfall, Norway may have to buy electric power from neighboring countries. Many of the power plants are located inside mountains and so do not harm the landscape.

Opposite: **An oil production platform in the North Sea**

Diverse Norwegians

For centuries, Norwegians believed there were only two types of people in Norway—the Sami and the descendants of the invading Germanic tribes. The Sami are probably the original people who moved from Central Asia after the glaciers retreated. The Germanic tribes arrived later, moving into Norway through Denmark.

Most Norwegian people today are of Germanic origin, as are the Swedes and Danes. By reputation, these people—often called Nordic—are all tall, slender, blond, and blue-eyed. But, of course, that is not the case. Many other peoples with other characteristics have lived in Norway over the centuries, so a Norwegian is just as likely to be short, with dark hair and dark eyes.

Students in traditional regional clothes in the town of Drobak

Whatever they look like, though, Norwegians tend to regard themselves as one people, united by their pride in themselves and their traditions. Such a view kept them a separate people from the other nations that ruled them over the centuries. Today, though, things may be changing.

A Norwegian family enjoying the Syttende Mai parade

Thomas Hylland Eriksen, a Norwegian professor, wrote that Norwegians have an image of themselves as "mainly a nation of fishermen and farmers who live close to nature, they're simple and bucolic, and they grow awkward and clumsy when they travel abroad. This national-romantic image doesn't jibe with reality." Norwegians today are as cosmopolitan as any other

People attending Oslo National Theater

European people, and as more immigrants of totally different backgrounds come into this small country, the very definition of "Norwegian" may be changing.

The Sami People

Hunters and fishers followed animals northward as the ice cap retreated from Scandinavia. Sometimes they built houses with stone to stay a while. There are more Stone Age houses in Norway than elsewhere in Scandinavia. One entire settlement at least 9,000 years old has been found north of Tromsø.

The descendants of these early people are the Sami (from *Saemieh*, or "reindeer people"). Most are quite short, averaging only about 5 feet (1.5 m) tall. They are stocky and dark, but like many Scandinavians, they have blue eyes.

The Sami have long been nomadic people. They followed their herds of reindeer throughout the northern parts of Norway, Sweden, Finland, and the Kola Peninsula of Russia and knew no political boundaries. Today, the Sami are citizens of the country in which they make their permanent settlement. About two-thirds of the approximately 50,000 Sami live in Norway, especially in Finnmark. The Sami divide themselves into several groups, such as sea-Sami, forest-Sami, and moun-

Who Lives in Norway?	
Norwegians	96.3%
Danes	0.4%
Swedes	0.3%
British	0.3%
Pakistanis	0.2%
Americans	0.2%
Yugoslavians	0.2%
Iranians	0.2%
Others	1.9%

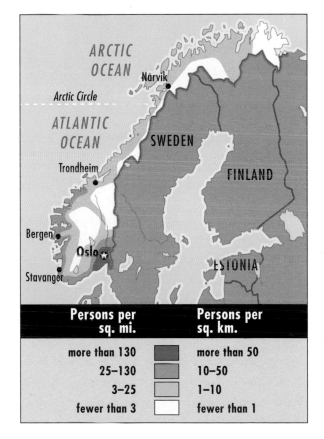

Persons per sq. mi.		Persons per sq. km.
more than 130		more than 50
25–130		10–50
3–25		1–10
fewer than 3		fewer than 1

Sami Clothing

Traditional Sami clothing, called *gakti,* was made of reindeer or seal hides, plus other furs. When the people started to acquire brightly colored cloth from outside traders, they began applying colorful pieces to their traditional clothing. Today, the people in different areas of Samiland feature different colors on their gakti.

Some people, especially children, wear large, star-shaped hats in winter. The Sami herders, who are continually on the move in the ice and snow, often line their reindeer-hide boots with grass for warmth. The Sami who sell crafts to tourists usually wear traditional clothing, but most Sami wear European-style clothing.

tain-Sami, but they all refer to themselves as the "reindeer people."

The Sami Today

In many ways, the only thing that has changed is that families own their own herds of domesticated reindeer instead of having to follow the wild herds. Reindeer herding is regarded by the national government as both an economic activity and a cultural activity for the Sami people. However, the reindeer habitat is shrinking and cannot support big herds. Many Sami must now find other ways to make a living.

Traditionally, several Sami family groups gathered into a cooperative arrangement called a *siida.* The leader of the siida made sure that everyone shared in the resources of the territory, which belonged to the siida as a whole.

For many decades, the government had an official policy of "Norwegianization." The people in Oslo thought it would benefit the Sami to live like other Norwegians. During those years, many Sami tradi-

tions were lost. Now, the Norwegian Constitution guarantees the Sami the right to assistance in preserving their culture.

The Sami in Norway have their own parliament, called the *Sametinget*, located in Karasjok, the capital of Samiland. This parliament cannot enact laws, but it protects the interests of the Sami. It also encourages young people to learn their language, which was outlawed for many decades until the 1950s.

Some Sami people make a living by herding reindeer.

The Sami parliament

Population of Major Cities	
Oslo	487,908
Bergen	223,100
Trondheim	143,746
Stavanger	104,322
Baerum	97,019

Norwegian street signs

Languages of Norway

Most Scandinavians originally spoke Old Norse, the language in which the sagas were written. It was used primarily after the Viking Era, from about 1100 to 1350, but was not spoken at all by 1500. The modern languages of Norwegian, Icelandic, and Faeroese (spoken on the Faeroe Islands off Iceland and Scotland) came from Old Norse.

As the minor partner in the Denmark-Norway union, Norway's language had no importance. Danish became the official language of written communication. The Norwegians still spoke their own language but, over the centuries, it took on characteristics of Danish.

The Sami languages are more closely related to Finnish than to Norwegian, but the dialects used by the people of Samiland are so different that two Sami from different regions often cannot understand each other.

In addition, there are small sections of far northern Norway where the people speak Finnish. These people fled into Norway from Finland in the mid-1800s to escape war.

Writing

The ancient Scandinavians had a method of writing called runes. Probably regarded as magical, runes made up an alphabet of twenty-four letters that could be shaped with twigs or sharp cuts into wood or bone. Runes, which were probably based on the Latin alphabet, may have been used as charms against evil or as memorials. The oldest runes discovered in Norway date from about A.D. 300.

When Christianity came to Norway, the Norwegians made some changes in the Latin alphabet to represent the sounds they make that didn't quite fit. The vowels æ, ø, and å are three examples. When alphabetizing, words or names that start with one of those vowels come after z. Several letters in our alphabet are not used in Norwegian—c, q, w, x, and z exist only in words that have come into Norwegian from foreign sources.

The Language Today

There are two forms of Norwegian, both of which are acceptable in Norway. Most people use *Bokmål*, meaning "book language." It is also called Dano-Norwegian because it is based on the language used when Denmark and Norway were united. However, the written language was deliberately changed to reflect the way people spoke.

The second form is *Nynorsk*, meaning New Norwegian, and sometimes called *Landsmål*. But, oddly, it's not newer. It's closest to the Old Norse languages used long ago. Nynorsk was developed in the mid-1800s when a Norwegian-language scholar named Ivar Aasen began studying the old dialects used in country areas.

Aasen didn't do this just because he thought it would be interesting, but because Norwegians were looking for a way to break their ties with Denmark. Most speakers of Nynorsk live in the eastern, more rural part of Norway and among the Sami. In Nynorsk, the name of Norway is *Noreg*. The phrase "I don't understand" is *Jeg forstår ikke* in Bokmål and *Eg forstår ikkje* in Nynorsk. People can readily understand both forms of

The Nature of Names

Once, families lived on the same island or on the same farm for many, many generations. It was customary for a man to take his father's first name and add "søn" to it to make a last name. "Anderssøn," for example, was the son of Anders. This way of naming became very confusing as the population increased, and most families have settled on one fixed last name. But this is the reason that there are so many Johnsons, Hansons, and the like.

Common Norwegian (Bokmål) Words and Phrases

du	you
hva	what
nå	now
God dag.	Good day.
Ha det.	Bye!
Tusen takk.	Thank you very much.
mor	mother
far	father
år	year
Gratulerer med dagen.	Happy birthday.

Counting to Ten

1	en	6	seks
2	to	7	sju
3	tre	8	åtte
4	fire	9	ni
5	fem	10	ti

the language. Each community is free to decide for itself which form of Norwegian the children will be taught as their primary language.

The Era of Immigration

A small ship called a sloop carried the first group of Norwegians to North America. They were seeking religious freedom, but later Norwegian emigrants were looking for something else.

Free Norwegians were allowed to vote as early as the time when Christianity came to Norway. This makes the nation one of the world's earliest democracies. However, even as recently as the late 1800s, a man had to own land in order to vote. At that time, the only way to acquire land was to leave Norway and go to a place where ownership of land was more easily achieved. For many Norwegians, that place was the United States.

During the era in which so many Norwegians emigrated to the United States, the population of Norway itself was not greatly reduced. Smallpox vaccinations were now widespread, and fewer people died from the disease. Along with better nutrition, vaccinations allowed people to live longer and to raise more children to adulthood.

The Incredible Nansen

He has been described as an "explorer, author, athlete, oceanographer, statesman, and laureate of the Nobel Peace Prize." Born on a farm near Oslo in 1861, Fridtjof Nansen became a champion cross-country skier and skater while still a teenager. At university, he took part in a research voyage into the Arctic Ocean, and oceans were never again very far from his mind.

Nansen's greatest expedition was aboard the *Fram,* which means *"Forward."* This was a boat he had specially built to withstand being crushed by ice. With provisions to last six years, he and twelve other adventurers let their hardy ship get locked into the Arctic pack ice in 1894. For three years they were out of contact with the world. While the ship appeared to be barely moving in the current that Nansen was certain flowed under the ice, he and a companion decided to try to reach the North Pole, hoping to become the first humans ever to do so. But they were ill prepared, and the weather was worse than they expected. That honor was left to others. In 1922, he won the Nobel Peace Prize for helping refugees after World War I.

Thor Heyerdahl, Modern Viking

In 1947, a Norwegian scientist set sail on a small, flimsy balsa-wood raft called the *Kon-Tiki.* Thor Heyerdahl and his crew of five left from South America to see if they could reach the island area called Polynesia in the Pacific Ocean on their fragile boat. Heyerdahl was hoping to show that the Polynesian islands could have been settled by South American Indians, whom Polynesian people resemble. The journey took three and a half months, and carried the intrepid sailors 5,000 miles (8,047 km). Heyerdahl's book about the trip, *Kon-Tiki,* was a worldwide best-seller. The fragile raft is on display in Oslo's Kon-Tiki Museum.

Heyerdahl was most interested in how ancient cultures could have spread. Long after his *Kon-Tiki* voyage, in a papyrus boat called *Ra* (right), he showed that ancient peoples of Africa and South and Central America could have met and shared knowledge.

Gods, Trolls, and Faith

THE VIKINGS BELIEVED THAT MANY DIFFERENT GODS AFFECTED their everyday lives. There were two families of gods, the Æsir and the Vanir. The Æsir gods lived in a fortress called Asgard. Among the Æsir were the prime gods, Odin and Thor (from whom we get the name Thursday). Odin's wife was Frigg, and their son was Balder. The god of war was Tyr. Odin and Thor had a companion named Loki, a trickster who could change his shape or appear as a woman.

Odin is the main Norse god of the Æsir family.

Odin was a complex figure—part wizard, part warrior, part poet. He was the Lord of the Slain, who controlled the fortunes of warriors, decreeing whether they lived or died during battle. It was the ambition of a Viking warrior to die with honor, knowing that he would join Odin in Valhalla. The Valkyries, young, beautiful, armor-wearing women, selected the dying warriors to take to Valhalla. The name *Valkyrie* means "Chooser of the Slain."

The Norse god Thor with his magical hammer

The warriors didn't expect just to live happily ever after, eating and drinking in Valhalla. They were certain that Odin required their help in the great battle of the gods that was to come, a battle called *Ragnarøk,* meaning "Twilight of the Gods." It would be a battle against all the evil of the world, in the form of giants and trolls and demons.

The common people probably did not worship Odin, or even pay much attention to him. They called on Thor for help in time of need, for everything from success in battle to a request for rain for their crops. The sound of thunder was made by Thor's chariot.

The other family of gods—the Vanir—ranked below the Æsir. The Vanir played a more direct role in the lives of people than the Æsir did. Brother and sister gods—Frey and Freya—had power over fertility, both in agriculture and human life. But Freya was also a goddess of war, who took half of the Vikings who died in battle away from Odin and brought them to her fortress.

Faith in a Drum

The Sami believe in many gods, especially in natural things. Their spiritual leader, or shaman, is called the *noaid.* He gets messages from the gods by drumming on a special drum that is marked with symbols. A small marker is placed on the drum head, and as he drums, the marker moves around from the vibration. It comes to rest pointing to a symbol that conveys the gods' message, which may concern health or the future.

Once Upon a Time...

Some of the Viking leaders who spent a long time in England came to accept Christianity while they were there. They brought back to Norway a new religion whose followers worshiped a single god. However, the pagan belief in warrior gods lingered for several centuries. Tales of lesser spirits—such as trolls—who made life difficult for good Christians, continue into today's storybooks. Trolls can be huge and fearsome or small and evil. In either size, they can be outsmarted by "three billy goats gruff."

Trolls have been described as "explaining the unexplainable." If something small and annoying, or even grandly catastrophic happens, "accident" is not always a satisfactory explanation. It's much more satisfying to say that a troll did it. The trolls' realm is nighttime. In sunlight, they may turn to stone—or even explode. Trolls aren't easy to kill, if only because they have several heads, and if one is chopped off, a new one grows.

Hidden Folk and Ghosts

The *huldrefolk* are human-looking "hidden folk" who have lives similar to ours, but they live underground. Some lakes belong strictly to the huldrefolk, and anyone wanting to fish in them needs to get permission—though where to get it is not certain.

If a person visits the huldrefolk, he may find, on returning to the "real" world, that though he thinks he's been gone only an hour, the real time may have been months or years. But if a person eats or drinks with huldrefolk, she may be lost to the real world forever.

Religions of Norway

Evangelical Lutherans	87.8%
Other Protestants and Catholics	3.8%
Nonreligious	3.2%
Unknown (includes Buddhists and Muslims)	5.2%

The Kraken, as Seen by the Eye of Imagination by Edward Etherington

Beware, too, the many ghostly figures of Norwegian legend. Among them is the *draug*, the headless ghost of a sailor whose body was thrown into the sea without a Christian burial. He sails the seas doing sinister deeds and luring unlucky sailors to him. The *kraken* is a giant sea creature whose presence determines whether there are fish to be caught in the area. And many people believe that Lake Mjøsa has a sea serpent in it.

Farm Spirits

Farmers have several legendary creatures to help them out. A *gardvord*, for example, is a spirit—perhaps a ghost—who keeps evil away from farms. A farmer who wants his gardvord to stay and work provides a special bed for it.

Another helpful spirit on a farm is a *nisse*, a tiny, bearded fellow who usually wears a red cap and looks like an elf. He is quite tiny and has no thumbs, so it's hard to see how much help he can be to a farmer. Luckily, a nisse needs to be fed only once a week, preferably with a special pudding called *rømmegrøt*, and preferably on Thursdays.

It's a puzzle why Thursday should be important, but it's recommended that a person who wants to learn to play the fiddle should contact a *grim*, or *fossegrim*, on a Thursday. This spirit is a musician who plays the fiddle quite beautifully, especially near mills and waterfalls. Many a fine Norwegian violinist claims to have learned from a grim.

Ancient Churches

In pre-Christian Norway, pagan gods were worshiped in a building called a *hov*. When the king decided the people should become Christian, the hov were torn down and replaced by wooden buildings called stave churches. Starting about 1100, many hundreds of stave churches were built, but only about thirty stand in their original locations today. The oldest existing stave church in Norway is at Urnes. It was built about 1070, but the materials in it had probably been used at least a hundred years earlier.

This church at Urnes is the oldest existing stave church in Norway.

The Nidaros Cathedral in Trondheim

A stave is half of a tree trunk that serves as the corner post of a wall, to which slender strips of timber are fastened. The technique allowed the Norwegians to build churches with several steep roofs that shed snow and made them seem incredibly high on the inside.

In contrast to the beautiful little stave churches is the great stone Nidaros Cathedral in Trondheim. The site of royal coronations and burials, it is the largest medieval building in Scandinavia. It is also the northernmost medieval cathedral.

The Saintly King

Norwegians were reluctant to give up their old gods until King Olav Haraldsson died in battle in 1030. Olav (originally called Olav the Stout) had converted to Christianity in 1013 after he invaded France. As king, he demanded that Norwegians become Christians—they had to be baptized or be killed.

Miracles began to happen almost immediately after Olav's death, when a wounded follower threw himself on the king's body and the man's wounds were healed. Olav's body was taken to Trondheim and the miracles continued. Within a year after his death, Olav was declared a saint, and he became the patron saint of Norway. Nidaros Cathedral is built on the site of this king's grave. Saint Olav's Day is celebrated on July 29.

Turning Protestant

Christian III of Denmark-Norway brought the Protestant Reformation to Norway in the mid-1500s, only a few years after Martin Luther led the movement that made many Christians break away from the Roman Catholic Church. Lutheranism, now the established religion in Norway, was accepted by most people very quickly.

For several centuries, Norwegians were required to belong to the Lutheran Church. If they were not active in the church, they could not hold office and were even punished. They had to be married in the church, and they could not be buried without the church ritual.

Some Quakers objected to these rituals. Quakers believe people can commune directly with God without ritual and priests. The Quakers of Stavanger listened to the stories of Cleng Peerson. Peerson had spent several years in the United States, where freedom of religion was the law. On July 4, 1825, fifty-two Norwegian Quakers and sympathizers left Stavanger on the sloop *Restoration*. Only one-fourth as big as the *Mayflower*, the *Restoration* should never have made it across the Atlantic, but these Quakers arrived safely and settled in northern New York.

Ten years later, more Norwegians began emigrating to North America in organized groups. And ten years after that—1845—Norway offered all its people religious freedom.

Today's Churches

Today, 88 percent of the Norwegian people belong to the Lutheran Church of Norway, though probably not even half of them attend church regularly. About 20 percent of Norwegian children attend Sunday school and church. For them, confir-

A church and graveyard at the tip of Innvik Fjord

mation is an important occasion. This is a time of solemnity for the person confirming the faith, and of celebration at becoming a young adult.

Norway also has congregations of Lutheran Free Church (which functions outside the structure of the state church), Anglicans, Baptists, Roman Catholics, Methodists, and Pentecostals, among others. There are a growing number of Muslims in Norway, especially among refugees who have come to live there.

The 1814 Constitution contained a provision that Jews were not allowed into Norway. That law was repealed in 1831, and some Jews began to come from Russia, where they were being massacred. Their numbers were never large, however.

About 1,400 Jews lived in Oslo when the Nazis—with their determination to destroy all Jews—arrived in 1940. Half of the Norwegian Jews were imprisoned in Nazi concentration camps, where almost all of them died. Others had their property taken away by the Nazi-controlled government. In 1998, the Norwegian government proposed a plan to compensate all the Jews they could and to contribute to a worldwide fund helping Jews all over the world.

Christmas

Christmas is a very important day of the year for Norwegians. Actually, it's more than just a day, it's a long, wonderful time, with activities planned for many days, at least until January 6, when the three wise men are said to have arrived with gifts for the infant Jesus.

A Norwegian family carrying their Christmas tree home

With its huge forests of spruce and pine, Norway has perhaps more Christmas trees available than any other country in the world. They are usually decorated with ornaments made of straw, and they often have strings of tiny Norwegian flags on them, along with strings of lights.

Christmas parties are held after Christmas Day, instead of before. They usually feature foods that are all white, such as *lutefisk*, *lefse*, and creamed potatoes.

On Christmas Eve, a farmer's nisse is given a bowl of rømmegrøt to persuade him not to play tricks. If it is gone in the morning, the nisse has agreed to behave for the next year—but don't count on it!

Important Religious Holidays

Epiphany	January 6
St. Canute Day	January 13
St. Hans (John's) Day	June 24
St. Olav's Day	July 29
Christmas	December 25

A Christmas dinner of trout and salmon

Thriving in the Outdoor World

As might be expected, Norway's greatest sports activity involves snow and ice. Skiing probably began about 6,000 years ago in the far north of Scandinavia, started by clever people looking for an easy way to get around in their snowy land. A rock carving made at least 4,000 years ago and found in northern Norway shows a human figure on skis.

Until about 1850, skis were fastened to the boot by leather straps around the toes, which let the skis come off quite easily. This restricted what could be done on skis. Then, Sondre Norheim, a native of Telemark, made bindings of willow and other branches that could be soaked in water and allowed to harden into position around the foot. This let the foot move and turn without the ski falling off. Skiing was suddenly revolutionized and became a sport.

From then on, most milestones in the history of skiing were made in Norway, including the first written manual, the first ski club, the first ski-jump competition, and the first cross-country ski race. Because skiing originated and flourished in Norway,

Schoolchildren taking cross-country skiing lessons

many of the terms used in international skiing are Norwegian. These include *slalom*, *Telemark ski*, *christiania* (*christi* for short), and *birkebeiner*.

Downhill skiing is called Alpine skiing. The mountains of Norway are not terribly high, so downhill skiing is not as dramatic as it is in the Alps. Some good vertical drops can take a skier by surprise, though.

Participants in the well-known Birkebeiner cross-country ski race

More important in Norway is cross-country skiing. It uses a lighter ski that can be moved as if a person were walking or running. The advantage of cross-country is that anyone can do it, almost anywhere—in a backyard, on urban streets, or along a hiking trail. A major cross-country race called the Birkebeiner has been held in Norway for centuries. Thousands of participants race from Lillehammer to Rena.

Skiing for the blind was invented in Norway. Special ski runs and trails have electronic equipment along the sides that send out radarlike audible signals that change as the skier moves.

The First and the Greatest

Figure skater Sonja Henie was born in Oslo (then called Christiania) in 1912, the daughter of a fur seller who had also been a world-class bicycle champion. Sonja won her first competition when she was eight years old and became Norway's national champion at ten. She startled spectators by doing athletic jumps. Women were not expected to perform leaps and jumps—it wasn't ladylike!

The little blonde from Oslo won her first world figure-skating championship at age thirteen and went on to win nine more times, holding the position of champion of the world from 1927 to 1936. She also won the gold medal at the Winter Olympics three times.

Henie turned professional and moved to the United States. She starred in several movies about skating and was almost as popular in the late 1930s as Shirley Temple. A fine businesswoman, this tiny skater from Oslo went on to become one of the most financially successful athletes ever. She built a modern art center called Blommenholm, near Oslo. Henie told her own story in *Wings on My Feet*. She died in 1969.

Because there are places in Norway where the snow never melts, avid skiers can ski in the summer. On a sunny day, they can ski in bathing suits, but the snow and ice are still cold.

As in the United States, Canada, and many other countries, snowboarding, which uses just one wide board instead of skis, has become popular. Many ski hills are shaped to make this sport more challenging.

Dogsledding on a frozen river in Finnmark

A different way of traveling over ice and snow is by dogsled. Dogsled racing is very popular in Scandinavia. The Finnmark Race is a dogsled race comparable to the famed Ididarod in Alaska. Lasting

A New Way to Explore

Over the Christmas season of 1996–1997, Norwegian adventurer Børge Ousland made the 1,675-mile (2,696-km) journey across the Antarctic continent alone, the first person ever to do so. He strapped parachutelike sails to his body and let the strong Antarctic winds push him along on his skis as he pulled a sled loaded with more than 400 pounds (181 kg) of supplies.

several days, it takes teams of sleds, dogs, and humans along an old mail route across the Finnmark plateau.

Snowmobiles are also increasingly popular. Many people have vacation huts in the forests, where they enjoy following trails by snowmobile. Many Sami travel their far northern land by snowmobile.

Sports in the City

City living doesn't stop Norwegians from participating in sports. Three-fourths of the city of Oslo consists of parks, forests, and open fields. So it's easy for the residents of the other one-fourth of the area to reach open spaces.

In 1952, the Winter Olympics brought skiers, skaters, and other winter athletes from around the world to Oslo, which was proud to show how well the city had recovered from World War II. The opening and closing ceremonies were held at Bislett Stadium.

Also in Oslo is Holmenkollen ski jump, considered one of the most terrifying jumps in the world, and definitely the oldest. Originally con-

Bislett Stadium

To the sports-minded, the heart of Oslo is Bislett Stadium. Opened in 1922, it is set in a busy neighborhood and has all the drawbacks of an old stadium. The most significant drawback is that the stadium has only six lanes instead of the usual eight for track and speed-skating events. But many world records have been broken in the venerable building.

Norwegian runners and skaters who trained at Bislett have made names for themselves. Grete Waitz won the New York City marathon race nine out of ten years between 1978 and 1988. Ingrid Kristiansen held the women's marathon world record after 1985. Hjalmar Andersen won three gold medals in speed skating.

structed in 1892, it was rebuilt for the 1952 Olympics. It is used now only for the national ski-jump championships.

Hege Riis played for Norway in the 1995 Women's World Cup game against the United States.

When the Weather's Warmer

Soccer—called football in many countries, including Norway—has been popular in Norway since its beginnings around the world. The Norwegian Football Federation was started in 1902. Norwegian teams made it into the World Cup competition in 1938, 1994, and 1998. In 1936, the Norwegian Olympic team won a bronze medal, the best Norway has ever done in international soccer competition. The Norwegian women are also

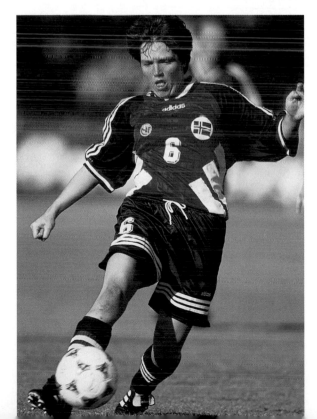

Olympics at Lillehammer

Skiers, skaters, and other athletes from sixty-six nations came to Norway in 1994 for the Seventeenth Winter Olympics (above, left), held in Lillehammer, north of Oslo. The opening ceremony was held at Lysgardsbakken Ski Jumping Arena. Norwegian skier Stein Gruben carried the torch down the steep ski jump to light the Olympic flame.

Norwegian athletes really showed their mettle. Norway came in first, with the most gold medals, ten of them. Johann Olav Koss (above, right), a speed skater, set world records in three long-distance events.

In 1998, Lillehammer opened an Olympics Museum. It covers the story of the modern Olympic Games from their founding in 1896 to the 1994 Winter Games.

world-class. In 1995, Norway won the Women's World Cup in soccer, beating Germany.

Most Norwegians live within a few miles of a lake, a fjord, the water between islands, or even the ocean itself. Swimming is a popular sport in water that is kept reasonably warm by the North Atlantic Current. Fishing is just as popular (especially fly-fishing on trout streams) for sport and an occasional meal. Because so many towns are built around harbors, sailing is also a common activity.

Fishing for trout

Winter or summer, the forests and mountains of Norway draw Norwegians from the cities and visitors from around the world for the fairly new sport called "orienteering." Participants are given maps of an area they don't know. Using their own knowledge of directions and maps, they run to a variety of checkpoints and, finally, to the goal.

Music Makers

Norwegians have always been music makers—perhaps as a way to pass the time when the sun is gone from the sky. Their folk songs and dances have gone around the world as Norwegians emigrated.

Lene Crawford Nystrøm, a native of Toensberg, sings in the Scandinavian rock group Aqua.

When people in an isolated valley got together, one of the activities they most enjoyed was dancing. It was a way of showing their joy in breaking out of isolation, at least for a little while. There are many different forms of folk dances because each valley was cut off from the next, and gradually, over decades, the dances changed in different ways.

The Sami people have a special haunting type of song called *joik*, which is gradually becoming loved by wider audiences. Mari Boine, who was born in the Sami village of Gamehhis-njarga, is a singer who has recorded a number of albums of traditional and popular music that sell worldwide.

Today's popular music is part of the music of Europe. Norway regularly sends competitors to the Festival of San Remo (Italy), to which European countries send songs and performers each year. One Scandinavian group called Aqua features Norwegian Lene Crawford Nystrøm. In 1999, the group became a big hit in the United States.

The *lur*, which some people identify as Norway's national symbol, is a bronze horn that may be as long as 8 feet (2.5 m).

Fiddle-dee-dee

Several different folk instruments were used traditionally to play the music for folk dancing. One of them, the Hardanger fiddle (above), or *hardingfele,* is now the official folk instrument of Norway. It has a shorter neck than the familiar violin, and it has eight strings instead of four. Four of the strings are played, and the other four vibrate in response, setting up a droning sound that has been compared to the drone of a bagpipe.

Although it may have been used in rituals, it also relayed messages between valleys, or between a farmhouse and the herders far away.

Ole Bull, a native of Bergen, was a violinist and composer who became world famous. Although he's not often remembered today, he discovered one of Norway's greatest composers. Bull met Edvard Grieg in Bergen when Grieg was only fifteen. Bull urged the boy's parents to send him to Germany for expert training in musical composition.

When Grieg returned to Norway, he began to write music that evoked his love of Norway, its beauty, and its old folklore, leading him to be called Norway's national composer. Many pieces reflect the splendor, solitude, and tranquillity of his nation's mountains. Among his most famous compositions is *Peer Gynt,* written to accompany Henrik Ibsen's play of the same name.

The Famed Playwright

Henrik Ibsen, a native of Skien, was born in 1828 to a family that met hard times and was never able to accept its change of fortune. One of the world's great playwrights, Ibsen wrote plays, including *A Doll's House, An Enemy of the People,* and *The Wild Duck,* that were attacks on the superior attitudes of the middle class.

Ibsen was only twenty-three when he was appointed director of a theater started by Ole Bull in Bergen. He began to produce a play every year, based primarily on Norway's Viking heritage. Unfortunately, those early plays were not popular with audiences. Ibsen moved to Christiania (now Oslo), and then abroad, where he lived on a small grant from the Norwegian government. There, he wrote plays that left a lasting impression.

One of Ibsen's most famous plays—which Norwegian composer Edvard Grieg made even more famous—was *Peer Gynt.* This play, written in poetry, called on the great legends and myths that the Norwegian people love.

The Painters

Norwegians are known worldwide for the beautiful painting of decorative objects called *rosemaling* (rose painting). This rural art consists of painting flowers, scrolls, and curlicues in bright colors on virtually any wooden household object. Patterns have been handed down in families for generations, and new ones are continually being created.

Probably the most famous Norwegian painter is Edvard Munch, born in Løten in 1863. His parents died when he was

The Scream by Edvard Munch

The City and the Sculptor

Gustav Vigeland, a native of Mandal, began sculpting as a young boy. He became enamored with huge, monumental sculptures. He persuaded the city of Oslo to let him fill a large park with his statues. In return, the city gave him a place to live and work.

Vigeland began his work in 1921. By his death in 1943, he had created 1,600 figures, all nude, set in about fifty groups around 100 acres (40.5 ha) in Oslo's Frogner Park, now called Vigeland Park. They show human beings at all stages of life and in all moods. Perhaps the most famous of the figures is *The Angry Boy*, a huge toddler stamping his foot in anger. The centerpiece is a 55-foot (17-m) monolith—a single piece of stone with numerous life-sized writhing human figures. Vigeland worked thirteen years on this sculpture.

Thriving in the Outdoor World **113**

Sigrid Undset

young, and in much of his work he used curvy lines to represent emotions about love and death. Munch gave the city of Oslo thousands of his paintings, which are on display in the Munch Museum in Oslo. One of his most famous paintings is *The Scream*, painted in 1893. It is often regarded as a symbol of the anxiety experienced by people living in the twentieth century.

Nobel Prize–Winning Writers

Bjørnstjerne Bjørnson, the author of Norway's national anthem, was one of Norway's great writers. He used historical images from the sagas in the anthem and his other poetry. This native of Kvikne was a poet, novelist, journalist, dramatist, theatrical producer, and politician. His writing brought him the Nobel Prize for Literature in 1903. He was the first Norwegian to be so honored, but not the last.

Like Ibsen and Bjørnson, novelist Sigrid Undset called on the folklore and history of Norway for much of her inspiration. She is most famous for *Kristin Lavransdatter*, a three-book story of a

Norwegian woman in medieval times. Undset was awarded the 1928 Nobel Prize for Literature, primarily for these books. Norwegian actress/director Liv Ullmann made the trilogy into a movie.

Between Bjørnson and Undset, another talented Norwegian, Knut Hamsun (his real name was Pedersen), won the Nobel Prize in 1920. Hamsun, who was raised in the distant Lofoten Islands, wrote novels about the struggle of individuals against society.

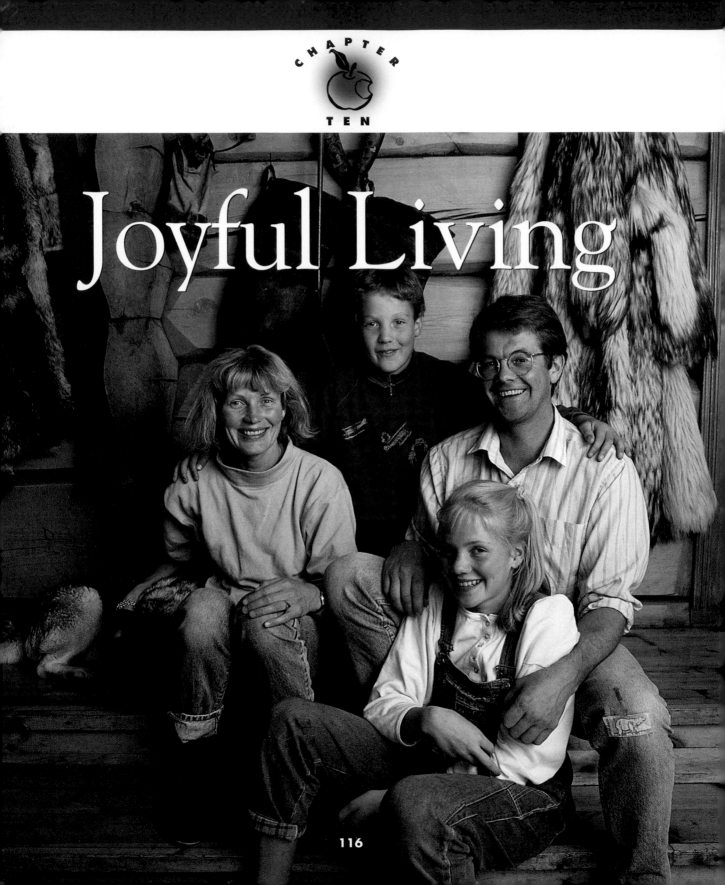

Joyful Living

Children dressed in traditional clothes proudly hold the Norwegian flag.

U NTIL THE TWENTIETH CENTURY, MOST Norwegians lived rural lives, with families isolated from one another except for the occasional planned gathering. A family had to be self-sufficient, growing its own food and making its own tools and clothing. Some farms in Norway have been in existence for almost 2,000 years.

Because of the farms' isolation, events that drew people together were very important. Everyone excitedly anticipated them. Weddings in rural areas, for example, were three- or four-day affairs, with music and dancing and plenty to eat.

Bunader for Weddings

One of the most striking sights at a Norwegian wedding is the costumes of the participants and guests. They often wear their *bunader*, or Norwegian national costumes, which are based on what people wore in the past.

A man's *bunad* starts with dark pants and a vest or jacket. A woman wears a dark full skirt, apron, and bodice. These basic items are varied by the designs of elaborate embroidery, the special beading, and even the shape of the hat, depending on what part of the country they came from. Caps and scarves are an important part of bunader. Traditionally, a person could tell whether a woman was married or unmarried by what she wore on her head. The cap may be changed as part of the wedding ceremony.

Opposite: **A Norwegian farm family**

A typical Norwegian wooden farmhouse with a sod roof

Farms and Cities

A traditional Norwegian wooden farmhouse was constructed with a sod roof. Sod, the upper part of soil in which grass grows, is filled with roots that hold the dirt together. It can be cut in strips and laid to form a roof. Even today, it isn't unusual to see a goat happily munching on the grass growing on top of a house.

Near the main farmhouse might be storehouses called *stabbur*. Fairly small, they are raised on stones or wooden posts to keep rats away from the grain. They are usually narrow at the bottom and wider at the top. Even today, stabbur are used to store dried meats.

118 *Norway*

Most farms had enough land so that their livestock could be sent up into the mountains to the *seter*, or outer farm, for the summer. The herder—usually a family member—lived in a small house called a *hytte* during the summer.

Hytter are not just a thing of the past or of rural life, however. Many city dwellers have their own huts in the mountains or along the coast where they can live rustically and just enjoy the countryside for a few days.

Norway's cities are not large, but they offer all the amenities of much larger cities—great shopping, theater, nightlife, museums and galleries, and, of course, convenience. Just as important, though, is the fact that Norwegian cities incorporate as much nature as possible in their designs. Water, mountains, ski runs, and open parkland are as vital to the Norwegian way of life as streets and high-rises.

The Skarven Café is a popular nightspot in Tromsø.

Going to School

Norway established a national program of education in 1827. Each child was required to attend a few years of primary school starting at age seven. Today, the law requires ten years of schooling.

The ten years of compulsory education are divided into the first six years, called *barntrinnet,* and the four higher years, called *ungdomstrinnet.* After that, any young person who wants to can go on to an additional three-year program called upper secondary, or *videregående skole.* This may involve training in an occupation, or it may be preparation for college.

A primary school classroom

The university at Oslo

All Norwegian children are required to learn English and at least one other language. They also receive religious education as part of their regular schooling, although children who do not belong to the Church of Norway attend alternative classes.

Education is free for Norwegians through the university level. There are many small colleges, but only four full universities. They are located at Oslo, Bergen, Trondheim, and Tromsø, which has the northernmost university in the world.

Sami children have been taught in their own language since the 1970s if their parents request it. Otherwise, they learn in Norwegian. Information about the Sami has also been added to the curriculum at Norwegian schools so that the Sami people will no longer be so isolated. In 1989, with the encouragement of the Samiting, Norway opened a college to teach in the Sami language.

Opposite: **Boats are used for transportation and recreation in Norway.**

A *Russ* to Celebrate

Young Norwegians graduating from upper secondary school spend three weeks playing and having fun in a celebration called *Russ*. The name comes from the word for the color red, which traditionally was the color of the graduation gown of a person going on to university. But any color goes now, as well as just about any kind of tricks on favorite teachers, parades through the town, and middle-of-the-night serenades. The new graduates can do whatever they want as long as they don't hurt people or damage property. And the people in the town get to enjoy it all.

Traveling

Throughout most of Norway's history, the only public transportation was by boats moving north or south along the coast. For a hundred years or more, regular coastal steamers have traveled the 1,200 miles (1,931 km) from Bergen to Kirkenes, the last stop before Russia's Kola Peninsula. The round trip takes twelve days.

The first rail line in Norway was built in 1854 by members of the Stephenson family, who were English railway developers. The little line went from Oslo to Eidsvoll, where passengers could connect with the boat service that ran northward along Lake Mjøsa. Oslo and Bergen were connected in 1909 by a railway going through spectacular scenery, pulling together different parts of the country by land for the first time.

Norway's new major airport is Gardermoen, which opened in 1998. It is about twice as far from Oslo as the older airport of Fornebu, but fast trains carry travelers into downtown Oslo in about twenty minutes. Norway is a partner in SAS, the Scandinavian airline.

National Holidays in Norway

New Year's Day	January 1
Labor Day	May 1
Constitution Day	May 17
Midsummer Eve	June 23
United Nations Day	October 24

Getting the News

The entire country, including Finnmark, is connected by radio, television, computers, and newspapers. Radio and television were run by the Norwegian Broadcasting Corporation for many years, but private ownership has now outstripped the government stations and channels. Radio is a primary source of communication in rural areas.

The two most popular daily newspapers are *VG* (which stands for *Verdens Gang*) and *Dagbladet. Dag og Tid* is a weekly newspaper published in Nynorsk. There are several Sami-language newspapers and magazines, and even some television programs.

Medical Care

Norway has a strong system of social services. The citizens' medical care is paid for by the national government, and the hospitals are run by the state, counties, or municipalities. As part of the medical-insurance program, people who are unable to work receive pay. New parents—both women and men—receive almost their full pay for staying home to take care of a newborn baby.

Because of its geography, many places in Norway have too few people to support all the medical services that city people enjoy. The Norwegians take care of this by telemedicine, meaning that a nurse or other person in a distant valley can talk to qualified medical help far away and be shown by television what to look for or how to treat a patient.

Norwegians have one of the longest life expectancies in the world. The average man lives to be 74.8 years old, and the average woman to be 80.7 years old.

Eating Norwegian

Many typically Norwegian foods are enjoyed in Norwegian communities all over the world. Some of these traditional foods were developed from the need to preserve food through the long winter. *Gravlaks*, for example, is salmon that has been soaked in a seasoned salt for a long time. This is sliced thin and often eaten as one of the toppings for open-faced sandwiches called *smørbrød*. These sandwiches are served at several meals, as well as part of a fancier buffet called a *koldt bord*.

Seafood is popular in Norway.

Norwegians eat seafood frequently because it is so available. Cod—called *torsk* by the Norwegians—is the basis for many meals. Every market in every coastal town has cod to sell. Herring is served in many different ways, too.

Grøt is a simple porridge made by boiling milk for a long time and whipping flour into it. *Rømmegrøt* is the fancy, special-occasion version of

Lutefisk

One way of serving cod is either loved or hated by most Norwegians. Few people are neutral on the subject of *lutefisk*. This is a dried codfish that has been soaked in lye, a very strong chemical, which changes its texture. It is then soaked again in water to remove the chemical. Lutefisk is boiled and served with potatoes—perhaps with *lefse,* a Norwegian potato pancake—and a vegetable. It is often regarded as a Christmas treat.

grøt, made with thick cream instead of milk. It can be made slightly salty for a main course, or sugar and cinnamon can be added for dessert.

Values for the Future

At the beginning of 1999, Prime Minister Kjell Magne Bondevik, who represents the Christian People's Party, appointed a Values Commission. The members were given the responsibility for guiding people to think about their values as individuals and as citizens of Norway. Bondevik hopes that after interviewing thousands of people around the country, the commissioners will be able to draw up a statement about the nation's beliefs for the twenty-first century.

The people involved in the Values Commission hope that the project will remind people of their basic values. These have been important to Norwegians throughout their history and have made Norway the comfortable, thoughtful, social democracy that it has become.

Timeline

Norwegian History

Norwegian Vikings gain islands near Scotland, control Ireland, found settlements in Iceland and Greenland, and take over territory of Normandy in France. — A.D. 800 – 1050

Harald Fairhair proclaims himself king of the Norwegians. — 800s

Olav Tryggvason (Olav I) brings Christianity to Norway. — 995

Norway goes through a period of civil war. — 1130 – 1217

Håkon IV is crowned king of a unified Norway. — 1217

The Black Death kills half of Norway's population. — 1349 – 1350

Norway, Sweden, and Denmark are united in the Union of Kalmar. — 1397 – 1523

Norway becomes a province of Denmark. — 1535 – 1814

Lutheranism becomes the established religion in Norway. — 1536

World History

c. 2500 B.C. — Egyptians build the Pyramids and Sphinx in Giza.

563 B.C. — Buddha is born in India.

A.D. 313 — The Roman emperor Constantine recognizes Christianity.

610 — The prophet Muhammad begins preaching a new religion called Islam.

1054 — The Eastern (Orthodox) and Western (Roman) Churches break apart.

1066 — William the Conqueror defeats the English in the Battle of Hastings.

1095 — Pope Urban II proclaims the First Crusade.

1215 — King John seals the Magna Carta.

1300s — The Renaissance begins in Italy.

1347 — The Black Death sweeps through Europe.

1453 — Ottoman Turks capture Constantinople, conquering the Byzantine Empire.

1492 — Columbus arrives in North America.

1500s — The Reformation leads to the birth of Protestantism.

Norwegian History

Norway's present-day borders are confirmed in a treaty with Sweden.	1751
Sweden gains control of Norway; Norwegians write a constitution; the king of Norway gives up the throne to the king of Sweden. Norway grants religious freedom.	1814
	1845
The Storting (the legislature) gains control of Norway's executive branch of government.	1884
Norwegians vote to become independent of Sweden.	1905
Norway remains neutral during World War I.	1914– 1918
Norway declares neutrality during World War II.	1939
German ships and troops occupy Norway; Vidkun Quisling sets up a fascist government in Oslo.	1940
Germany is defeated in World War II; the occupation of Norway ends. Norway joins the United Nations.	1945
Norway joins the North Atlantic Treaty Organization.	1949
The Nordic Council, made up of Norway, Sweden, Denmark, Finland, and Iceland, is formed.	1952
Norway becomes a member of the European Free Trade Association.	1959
Petroleum and natural gas are found under Norway's part of the North Sea.	1969
Gro Harlem Brundtland becomes Norway's first female prime minister.	1981
Norwegians change the Constitution so that a woman can inherit the throne.	1990
Norway rejects membership in the European Union.	1994

World History

1776	The Declaration of Independence is signed.
1789	The French Revolution begins.
1865	The American Civil War ends.
1914	World War I breaks out.
1917	The Bolshevik Revolution brings Communism to Russia.
1929	Worldwide economic depression begins.
1939	World War II begins, following the German invasion of Poland.
1957	The Vietnam War starts.
1989	The Berlin Wall is torn down, as Communism crumbles in Eastern Europe.
1996	Bill Clinton is reelected U.S. president.

Fast Facts

Official name: Kingdom of Norway

Capital: Oslo

Official language: Norwegian

A Sami child

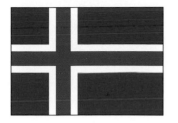

Norwegian flag

The Rauma River

Official religion:	Evangelical Lutheran
Year of founding:	1905
Founder:	Norwegian people
National anthem:	*Ja, vi elsker dette landet (Yes, We Love This Land)*
Government:	Constitutional monarchy
Chief of state:	King
Head of government:	Prime minister
Area and dimensions:	149,405 square miles (386,958 sq km) including island possesions; 1,089 miles (1,753 km), north to south; 270 miles (435 km) wide at its widest
Latitude and longitude of geographic center:	62° North, 10° East
Land and water borders:	Barents Sea to the north; Norwegian Sea to the west; Skagerrak to the south; Sweden to the east; Finland and Russia to the northeast
Highest elevation:	Galdhøpiggen, 8,100 feet (2,469 m) above sea level
Lowest elevation:	Sea level along the coast
Average temperature extremes:	14°F (–10°C) in the inland valleys in January; 63°F (17°C) in the south in July
Average precipitation extremes:	30 inches (76 cm) in the east; 80 inches (203 cm) in the west
National population (1998 est.):	4,419,955

Population of largest cities (1996 est.):

Oslo	487,908	Stavanger	104,322
Bergen	223,100	Bærum	97,019
Trondheim	143,746		

Famous landmarks:	*Akershus Castle, Fram* and *Kon-Tiki Museums,* and *Frogner Park* (Oslo)

Famous landmarks: *Akershus Castle, Fram* and *Kon-Tiki Museums,* and *Frogner Park* (Oslo)

Bryggen historic wharf (Bergen)

Hardangervidda National Park (near Geilo)

Jostedalsbreen (Europe's largest glacier)

Lillehammer Olympic Information Center

Nidaros Cathedral (Trondheim)

Norway's largest stave church (Heddal, west of Kongsberg)

Oddernes Church (near Kristiansand)

Trolls' Path and *Trolls' Wall* (Åndalsnes)

Industry: Mining is one of Norway's most valuable industries. Norway has Europe's largest offshore fields of petroleum and natural gas and Europe's largest deposits of titanium ore. Manufacturing is another leading Norwegian industry, with half of the country's factories located in and near Oslo. Petroleum products, chemical products, machinery, processed foods, and wood, pulp, and paper products are Norway's leading manufactured goods.

Currency: The krone (kroner is the plural) is Norway's basic monetary unit. Early 2000 exchange rate: U.S.$1 = 7.99 kroner.

System of weights and measures: Metric system

Literacy rate (1996 est.): 100 percent

Common Norwegian words and phrases:

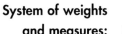

Adjø (ah-DYUR)	Good-bye.
brød (brur)	bread
God dag (goo DAHG)	Hello.
Hvor er . . .? (vorr ehr)	Where is . . .?

Currency

ja (yah)	yes
melk (mehlk)	milk
nei (nay)	no
Tusen takk. (TEWS-sehn-tahk)	Thank you very much.
Unnskyld. (EWN-shewl)	Excuse me.
Vær så god. (VEHR-soh-goo)	You're welcome.
vann (vahn)	water

Famous Norwegians:

Bjørnstjerne Bjørnson   (1832–1910)
Writer, Nobel Prize–winner

Gro Harlem Brundtland   (1939–   )
Former prime minister;
director of the World Health Organization

Edvard Grieg   (1843–1907)
Composer

Håkon VII   (1872–1957)
First elected king (1905–1957)

Sonja Henie   (1912–1969)
Figure skater

Thor Heyerdahl   (1914–   )
Scientist

Henrik Ibsen   (1828–1906)
Poet, playwright, dramatist

Trygve Lie   (1896–1968)
First UN secretary-general

Edvard Munch   (1863–1944)
Painter

Fridtjof Nansen   (1861–1930)
Explorer, statesman, Nobel Prize–winner

Vidkun Quisling   (1887–1945)
Traitor

Sigrid Undset   (1882–1949)
Writer, Nobel Prize–winner

Gustav Vigeland   (1869–1943)
Sculptor

Henrik Isben

To Find Out More

Nonfiction

▶ Heyerdahl, Thor, with Christopher Ralling. *Kon-Tiki Man: An Illustrated Biography*. San Francisco: Chronicle Books, 1990.

▶ James, Barbara. *Conserving the Polar Regions*. Austin, Tex.: Steck-Vaughn, 1991.

▶ Simon, Charnon. *Leif Ericksson and the Vikings*. The World's Greatest Explorers. Chicago: Children's Press, 1991.

▶ Sipiera, Paul P. *Roald Amundsen and Robert Scott*. The World's Greatest Explorers. Chicago: Children's Press, 1990.

Fiction

▶ Gaarder, Jostein. *Sophie's World*. Trans. Paulette Møller. New York: Farrar, Straus & Giroux, 1994.

▶ Rölvaag, O. E. *Giants in the Earth*. 1927. Reprint, New York: Harper Collins, 1999. A novel of Norwegian immigrants to the United States, first published in Norway.

▶ Undset, Sigrid. *Happy Times in Norway*. Trans. Joran Birkeland. New York: Alfred A. Knopf, 1942.

CD-Rom

▶ *Kon-Tiki Interactive*. Voyager, 1996.

Video

▶ *Norwegian Saga*. Associated Film Producers, 1992.

Internet Sites

▶ **The Sons of Norway**

http://www.sofn.com

Official site of the Sons of Norway, including useful information on heritage, outreach programs, history, and membership.

▶ **The Norway Online Information Service**

http://www.norway.org

An excellent compilation of information on the current political issues of Norway, including links to the tourist board, trade council, consulate, chamber of commerce, NATO, and many others.

▶ **Vikings: The North Atlantic Saga (National Museum of Natural History)**

http://www.nmnh.si.edu/arctic/features/viking/

Part of the Arctic Studies Center website, this link displays up-to-date information and recent findings about Viking life and includes information on exhibitions.

▶ **The Saami: People of the Sun and Wind**

http://www.sametinget.se/english/

History, culture, religion, and art of the Saami people. Includes contact information and background on the Sami parliament.

Organizations and Embassies

▶ **Embassy**
Royal Embassy of Norway
2720 34th Street, NW
Washington, DC 20008
(202) 333-6000

Index

Page numbers in *italics* indicate illustrations.

Meet the Author

J EAN F. BLASHFIELD delights in learning lots of fascinating, though not always important, things about places and the people who live in them. She says that when writing a book for young people, she's often as challenged by what to leave out of the book as by what to put in. She has long been particularly intrigued by Scandinavia, especially Norway. A lover of islands, she would like to visit as many as possible of Norway's huge collection of islands.

She has been a traveler since she first went on a college choir tour of Europe and made up her mind that she would go back. After developing the *Young People's Science Encyclopedia* for Children's Press, she kept that promise to herself and returned to London to live. That city became her headquarters for three years of travel throughout Europe. It was in London that she first began to write books for young people.

Since then, she has returned to Europe often (but not often enough! she says) while writing about ninety books, most of them for young people. She likes best to write about

interesting places, but she loves history and science, too. In fact, one of her big advantages as a writer is that she becomes fascinated by just about every subject she investigates. She has created an encyclopedia of aviation and space, written popular books on murderers and house plants, and had a lot of fun creating an early book on the things women have done, called *Hellraisers, Heroines, and Holy Women.*

She was the founder of the Dungeons & Dragons book department at TSR, Inc., and became avidly interested in medieval history. Nowadays she has trouble keeping the fantasy out of her medieval world, but she thinks she stuck to the facts in her coverage of Vikings in this book.

Jean Blashfield was born in Madison, Wisconsin, and has lived many other places. She has two college-age children, three cats, and two computers in her Victorian house in Delavan, Wisconsin. She has become an avid Internet surfer and is working on her own website, but she'll never give up her trips to the library and to other countries.

Photo Credits

Photographs ©:

Allsport USA: 107 bottom (Chris Cole), 108 right (Gerard Vandystadt);

AP/Wide World Photos: 70 (Greg Baker);

Archive Photos: 58 (Express Newspapers), 53 (Imperial War Museum), 27 (Popperfoto), 54 bottom, 105 top;

Bridgeman Art Library International Ltd., London/New York: 44 (AND76014/Viking ship, by H. Oakes-Jones/Private Collection), 94 (JF105440/The Kraken, as Seen by the Eye of Imagination, illustration from John Gibson's "Monsters of the Sea", 1887, engraving by Edward Etherington/Private Collection);

Brown Brothers: 114;

Bryan and Cherry Alexander Photography: 72, 76 (Wendy Else), 9, 28, 29, 33, 36, 51, 74, 82 top, 84, 85 top, 103, 105 bottom, 109, 119;

Corbis-Bettmann: 47 (Gianni Dagli Orti), 108 left (Reuters), 60 (Paul Thompson), 54 top, 55, 56, 89 bottom (UPI), 45, 62 bottom, 63 top, 71, 89 top, 112, 133;

Liaison Agency, Inc.: 62 top (Benainous-Deville), 98 (Frank Clarkson);

National Geographic Image Collection: 13 (Sisse Brimberg), 77 (Bill Curtsinger), 30, 31 bottom, 102 (George Mobley);

North Wind Picture Archives: 42, 43, 46, 91, 92;

Photo Researchers: 39 (B & C Alexander), 24 (Farrell Grehan), cover, 6 (Hubertus Kanus), 35 (Bud Lehnhausen), 81 (Porterfield/Chickering);

Randall Hyman: 113 bottom;

Scanpix Norge: 18 (Rolf M. Aagaard), 20 (BIA), 7 bottom, 12, 17, 34, 38, 63 bottom, 66, 67, 75, 78, 85 bottom, 86, 96 top, 100, 101, 104, 106, 107 top, 110, 120;

Superstock, Inc.: 113 top (National Gallery, Oslo, Norway/Bridgeman Art Library, London), 21, 118;

Tiofoto: 7 top, 23 (Bryan Alexander), 82 bottom (Ragnar Andersson), 37 (Torbjörn Arvidson), 79, 132 (Frank Chmura), 16, 19 (Lars Dahlström), 11, 131 (Chad Ehlers), 25 (Ove Eriksson), 40, 69, 121, 123 (Nils-Johan Norenlind), 117 (Lena Paterson), 125 (Björn Winsnes);

Tony Stone Images: 68 (Richard Elliott), 73 (Pal Hermansen), 80, 116 (Bob Krist), 137 (Martin Rogers), 90 (Hugh Sitton), 49 (Paul Souders), 8 (Tim Thompson);

Visuals Unlimited: 111 (D. Cavagnaro), 31 top (Derrick Ditchburn), 32 (Cheryl A. Ertelt), 2, 96 bottom, 130 (N. Pecnik).

Maps by Joe LeMonnier.